NEW DIRECTIONS FOR ADULT AND

Ralph G. Brockett, *University of Tennessee, Knoxville*
EDITOR-IN-CHIEF

Alan B. Knox, *University of Wisconsin, Madison*
CONSULTING EDITOR

The Emerging Power of Action Inquiry Technologies

Ann Brooks
University of Texas at Austin

Karen E. Watkins
University of Georgia

EDITORS

Number 63, Fall 1994

JOSSEY-BASS PUBLISHERS
San Francisco

THE EMERGING POWER OF ACTION INQUIRY TECHNOLOGIES
Ann Brooks, Karen E. Watkins (eds.)
New Directions for Adult and Continuing Education, no. 63
Ralph G. Brockett, Editor-in-Chief
Alan B. Knox, Consulting Editor

Microfilm copies of issues and articles are available in 16mm and 35mm, as well as microfiche in 105mm, through University Microfilms Inc., 300 North Zeeb Road, Ann Arbor, Michigan 48106-1346.

LC 85-644750   ISSN 0195-2242   ISBN 0-7879-9980-6

NEW DIRECTIONS FOR ADULT AND CONTINUING EDUCATION is part of The Jossey-Bass Higher and Adult Education Series and is published quarterly by Jossey-Bass Inc., Publishers, 350 Sansome Street, San Francisco, California 94104-1342 (publication number USPS 493-930). Second-class postage paid at San Francisco, California, and at additional mailing offices. POSTMASTER: Send address changes to New Directions for Adult and Continuing Education, Jossey-Bass Inc., Publishers, 350 Sansome Street, San Francisco, California 94104-1342.

SUBSCRIPTIONS for 1994 cost $47.00 for individuals and $62.00 for institutions, agencies, and libraries.

EDITORIAL CORRESPONDENCE should be sent to the Editor-in-Chief, Ralph G. Brockett, Department of Educational Leadership, University of Tennessee, 239 Claxton Addition, Knoxville, Tennessee 37996-3400.

Cover photograph by Wernher Krutein/PHOTOVAULT © 1990.

Manufactured in the United States of America. Nearly all Jossey-Bass books, jackets, and periodicals are printed on recycled paper that contains at least 50 percent recycled waste, including 10 percent postconsumer waste. Many of our materials are also printed with vegetable-based inks; during the printing process, these inks emit fewer volatile organic compounds (VOCs) than petroleum-based inks. VOCs contribute to the formation of smog.

Contents

EDITORS' NOTES

This volume describes strategies for learning through the use of action inquiry. It includes strategies used in such varied contexts as business, community development, and education. Some of these strategies, particularly those common to community development practice, have been used and written about by adult educators since the early 1970s. Others have become part of our work as adult educators as we have become increasingly involved in the practice of human resource development in organizations.

The term *action technology* has been adopted in this volume to include various strategies for learning through systematic inquiry. At the heart of all action inquiry is a recurring cycle of action, reflection, hypothesis, and revised or new action based on the reflections and hypotheses about what occurred in our previous action. In fact, action inquiry strategies can be defined as strategies for improving action through the use of systematic inquiry. Although many authors have offered adaptations of this cycle, the relationship between improved knowledge through action and improved action through reflection remains central to all action inquiry.

Although the action-reflection cycle is central to all action strategies, the strategies themselves vary. They are used in different contexts, for different purposes, with different modes of facilitation, and with different assumptions about learning. Those used within work organizations, for example, typically designate the improvement of organizational effectiveness or the improvement of individual practice as their broad overall goal. Those found most frequently within community contexts are often intended to make development efforts more appropriate to the community's perception of its needs and to help comparatively powerless groups become more powerful.

The role of the facilitator varies according to the amount of control he or she exercises. Frequently, in work organizations, the facilitator retains a substantial degree of control over the inquiry process. In community settings, however, where the purpose is more frequently to facilitate the shifting of control to participants, the facilitator strives to play an increasingly small role in the inquiry.

Finally, strategies differ according to whether the aim is adaptive or transformative change; these goals require participants to engage in different kinds of learning. Those seeking adaptive change use action strategies intended to improve the situation without altering its structure. Thinking or learning needed for this kind of change can be referred to as first order thinking (Elbow, 1986; Brooks, 1989) or single-loop learning (Ashby, 1965; Argyris, 1982). Those seeking transformative change use action strategies designed to completely restructure not only how they think about the problems they face, but also how they structure our social setting. The thinking or learning required for this kind of change can be referred to as second order thinking (Elbow,

1986; Brooks, 1989), critically reflective learning (Mezirow, 1991), or double-loop learning (Ashby, 1965; Argyris, 1982).

Ann Brooks and Karen Watkins, in Chapter One, place action technologies in a theoretical and historical context. Noting the increased interest in action inquiry, they discuss how it has changed over the years, what new issues have emerged in the practice of action inquiry, and the potential for action technologies to address the challenges of rapid change, diverse populations, and diminishing natural resources in innovative ways.

Chapters Two through Seven describe different approaches to action inquiry. Each chapter outlines the theory including the historical derivation of the approach, explains the "technology" or methodology used, and presents case illustrations of its use.

In Chapter Two, Judy O'Neil and Victoria Marsick describe a form of action learning that particularly emphasizes critical reflection on the part of the participants. Using examples from AT&T in the United States and Volvo Truck of Sweden, they show how critical reflection on managerial action can be used to develop more effective managers while solving organizational problems.

In Chapter Three, Max Elden and Reidar Gjersvik examine how action research is used to build both more democratic and productive workplaces in Norway. They make the point that the Norwegian model of action research emphasizes the need for the action research process to be democratic.

Karen Watkins and Tom Shindell, in Chapter Four, explore action science theory and practice as a means to transform individual and organizational action toward alignment with values. Because action science seems to call for a skilled facilitator, the authors provide specific examples that illustrate some of the challenges facilitators face.

In Chapter Five, the Group for Collaborative Inquiry and thINQ, two collaborative inquiry groups, describe efforts to unite practitioner and scholar for the purpose of contributing to the formal knowledge base of the adult education field. The authors give examples from their own experiences as inquiry groups.

In Chapter Six, Nod Miller describes how she used T-group technology and participatory action research to raise issues about economic inequalities. Through an intensive workshop format, participants developed their own economic system based on the real economic discrepancies among them.

In Chapter Seven, Carlos Torres and Gustavo Fischman describe popular education as a way of integrating action inquiry strategies into education with the intention of developing an education that changes rather than perpetuates the status quo. Drawing on examples from East Los Angeles and first nation people of Argentina, they explore the possibilities of popular education to facilitate social change.

In the last two chapters, Karen Watkins and Ann Brooks review the contributions of the authors of this volume and identify patterns and implications of their work. They compare the action technologies presented in this book, discussing their respective purposes, ideologies, potential problems, resource and facilitator requirements, and validity criteria. They also identify additional resources for readers who wish to explore these topics in greater detail, or who wish to contact groups of practitioners and scholars actively engaged in using and developing these technologies.

Ann Brooks
Karen E. Watkins
Editors

References

Argyris, C. *Reasoning, Learning, and Action: Individual and Organizational.* San Francisco: Jossey-Bass, 1982.

Ashby, W. R. *Design for a Brain.* New York: Wiley, 1965.

Brooks, A. K. "Critically Reflective Learning Within a Corporate Context." Unpublished doctoral dissertation, Teachers College, Columbia University, 1989.

Elbow, P. *Embracing Contraries: Explorations in Learning and Teaching.* New York: Oxford University Press, 1986.

Mezirow, J. *Transformative Dimensions of Adult Learning.* San Francisco: Jossey-Bass, 1991.

ANN BROOKS is assistant professor in the Adult Education and Human Resource Development Program, University of Texas at Austin, and a member of the Group for Collaborative Inquiry.

KAREN E. WATKINS is associate professor of adult education, University of Georgia, and former director of the graduate program in human resource development, University of Texas at Austin.

In this chapter, we explore the historical roots and current trends that have led to an increasing use of action technologies to enhance adult learning and facilitate organizational and social change.

A New Era for Action Technologies: A Look at the Issues

Ann Brooks, Karen E. Watkins

The age of action inquiry is upon us. After several decades of treating action and inquiry as separate endeavors to be carried out as distinct specializations, we are now questioning this traditional relationship. An increasingly complex and diverse world has challenged the capacity of traditional research to adequately address problems such as environmental degradation and depletion, relations among diverse groups and individuals, an increasingly global economy, and an increasingly large gap between the haves and the have nots combined with a shrinking middle class. Given the magnitude of the problems and the often overly specialized nature of research being done, both scholars and practitioners seem increasingly doubtful that control of research should remain solely in the hands of researchers or that theory should dictate how practitioners should practice and people should act. We are becoming less and less accepting of the idea that new knowledge should be produced exclusively by experts, and more and more sympathetic to the idea that research subjects and practitioners should know more about their lives and work and in a more insightful and complex way than do professional researchers.

In fact, action technologies have traditionally arisen in situations in which "expert" knowledge has been found less useful than "local" knowledge. As early as 1953, the Commissioner for Indian Affairs between 1933 and 1945 wrote: "We have learned that the action-evoked, action-serving, integrative and layman-participating way of research is incomparably more productive of social results than the specialized and isolated way, and also we think we have proved that it makes discoveries more central, more universal, more functional and more *true* for the nascent social sciences" (Corey, 1953, p. 293). However, in spite of this early insight, much of the writing about action inquiry comes from the perspective of researchers and social scientists. The technologies themselves reflect the passing fashions of academic thought, having used ritualized strategies of formal research such as surveys in the early days, and more participative interpretive strategies in recent years.

More enduring than the ways in which specific technologies are enacted have been the theories of experiential learning of scholars like John Dewey ([1938] 1963) and Eduard Lindeman ([1961] 1989). The notion that we learn from our experience through cycles of reflection and action is central to all of the action technologies. Action technologies systematize experiential learning into a process of knowledge construction usable by practitioners, citizen groups, and work groups alike. Unlike traditional research, they unite practice and theory in a way that privileges action and informal theory over formal theorizing and the reporting of research results. They use reflection on action as the basis for the generation and testing of informal theory. They restore control over learning about professional practice, cultural and community development, and work back to professional practitioners, community members, and workers; and they place "experts" in helping roles.

In the following section, we discuss how the control of scientists over the production and dissemination of knowledge led to a belittling of practical knowledge and a subsequent gap between theory and action, which action technologies hope to fill.

Historical Perspective on the Nature and Ownership of Knowledge

The history of research in the West is defined by two issues: (1) the nature of truth and knowledge and (2) control over the production and use of knowledge. These issues have been dealt with differently across the centuries. Until about the eighteenth century, Western people saw God as the source of all truth. The Catholic Church and its cadre of priests interpreted this truth for governments and individuals, thus controlling the production of knowledge. The Church was the final arbiter of what was truth and what was considered moral behavior, and it was the Church that sanctified the social order.

The Enlightenment brought an end to the church's control of knowledge as awareness dawned that, since reality could be observed and described empirically, anyone could know truth. Because reality was observable, everybody, not just priests, could know through their own empirical observations what was true and what was not. The age of science was born.

The beliefs of the Enlightenment released human beings, at least in principle, from the bondage of mystery and miracle held by the Catholic Church. However, it soon became clear that human observations are unavoidably colored by individual perspectives, or biases as they came to be called in science. To control these biases, the job of discerning truth through empirical observation became a highly specialized human task. The way in which one became qualified to learn about truth was through long and arduous training in the principles and practices of scientific research. The production of knowledge became ritualized as the scientific method, and universities and research organizations assumed the task of producing, cataloguing, and protecting the knowledge produced. University professors replaced priests as the controllers of knowledge. The highly ritualized and rigorous rules of research became the legitimate tool for discovering truth, and the arcane nature of research methodology lent the work of researchers and scholars a mystery and authority akin to that held by Catholic priests before the Enlightenment. The miracle of transubstantiation wherein wine is turned into blood and bread into flesh was matched by the generation of energy from atoms.

The transference of authority over the production and control of knowledge established a secular hierarchy similar to the hierarchy of the church that controlled knowledge in pre-Enlightenment days. The significance of such a hierarchy lies in what it does to our notion of learning. It institutionalizes learning in such a way that society considers credible only the learning that occurs in schools and universities. Other learning gets the less legitimate designation of "nonformal" or "informal" learning. Researchers and scholars assume the task of producing "formal" knowledge on behalf of all humankind. Others come to schools and universities to learn this formal knowledge. Thus, formal learning is in fact learning from others what they have learned—a kind of museum-work.

In professional practice, this means that practitioners learn from scholars basic knowledge, which they then apply to human problems. This means that expert scholars and practitioners are brought into communities as authorities to solve community problems. The problem of practice or action becomes that of implementing theory. The challenge for organizations like schools and development agencies becomes not how best to accomplish the work, but how best to act consistently with theory.

This imposition of theory as a template for good practice or effective development constituted a historical sleight of hand since formal theory transcended its definitional status of an unproven construction of how things work and ascended to the status of "truth." Theories came to be thought of as predictive; in other words, as models of "truth" that we could use to diagnose our problems and predict how to solve them. However, the difficulty practitioners encountered in "applying theory to practice" led practitioners and scholars alike to talk about the "theory-practice problem." Scholars were urged to make their work more relevant so that theory could be more directly applied to practice. In the field of education, "teacher-proof" curricula were developed in order to bypass practitioners altogether, imposing the most unmitigated form of theory possible on the real world of learners. In community development, experts were brought in to both define and solve the problems of "underdeveloped" nations and communities.

The late twentieth century has seen a skepticism toward universities and their priest-like scholars akin to the waning of the authority of the Catholic Church during the Enlightenment. We have seen the dark side of miracles such as atomic energy and technologies for efficiently mining the earth's resources. Similarly, we have begun to recognize that categories scientists used to describe the reality they observed were in fact arbitrary and observations were indeed "biased." Thus, the veil of mystery that shrouded science is evaporating as humankind adopts a critical stance toward grand solutions to particular problems and encompassing epic tales that gloss over uniqueness and block out smaller stories of more specific experiences.

Within this historical context, action technologies stand as the next logical step beyond the naive realism of natural social science. Action technologies reject the idea that one generalizable solution can fit multiple situations and establish a dynamic and ongoing inquiry into the particular. Theory becomes a learning tool for trying out solutions to local problems. By moving researchers from the role of objective observers into a collaborative relationship with research subjects, they share in rather than control the production of knowledge.

Similarly, action technologies incorporate passion and commitment into the research process. As Gramsci wrote, "The intellectual's error consists of believing that one can know without 'feeling and being impassioned'" (Forgacs, 1988, p. 349). In action technologies, there is no shelter in which researchers and co-researchers can hide from the deeply personal issues that force an uncomfortable element of researcher self-revelation. Action technologies open the door for researchers and co-researchers to seek insight into how their own assumptions came to be constructed. Researchers and co-researchers seek to learn to think about their own thinking. The result of these changes in the ways we think about research is that we gain the ability to pose the problems never posed before rather than solve problems the framing of which may have been problematic in the first place.

A History of Action Technologies

Since the early days of action research, numerous practitioners and scholars have developed new forms of action technologies to meet their own particular needs. However, Kurt Lewin is usually credited with formalizing the first kind of action technology in his article "Action Research and Minority Problems" (1946) in which he discusses action research as a strategy for improving intergroup relations. Lewin saw social change as occurring through the alteration of group culture rather than through individual change.

Action Research. In action research, a researcher works with a group to define a problem, collect data to determine whether or not this is indeed the problem, and then experiment with potential solutions to the problem. Data are then collected on the results of the experiment and fed back to the group. If it is determined that the solution was not successful, the group then works to redefine the problem, develop further experiments, and cycle again and again through this process of experimentation and reflection. The role of the action researcher is to guide data collection and analysis. Although this early model of action research had much of the research process under the control of the researcher, action research has developed over the years so that the relationship between the researcher and the subjects has become more collaborative. This is evidenced by the recent use of the term "co-researchers" to replace the older word "subjects."

At almost the same time as Lewin was working in the United States, a group of psychologists and social anthropologists in the United Kingdom carried out a number of experimental action-programmes having to do with personnel selection, treatment, and rehabilitation of wartime neurosis victims and returning prisoners of war. These became the basis for forming the Tavistock Institute of Human Relations, which defined action research in terms of getting "collaboration from members of an organization while trying to help them solve their own problems." Self-directed work teams in coal mines in England grounded in the socio-technical systems theory of researchers like Emery and Trist (Trist and others, 1963) emerged from this trend. Action research in this view, similar to that of Lewin and his colleagues in the United States, used a team of organizational members who had the power to effect a change and a behavioral scientist to change the social system.

Using action technologies within a more international arena, also in the 1940s, applied anthropologists developed a form of action research in response to problems of psychological warfare, intelligence, and the administration of occupied territories. This form was particularly sensitive to cultural issues. Applied anthropologists and sociologists such as Whyte (1991) as well as professionals in the field of economic development have used the sociocultural perspective brought by anthropology and sociology to help local populations find culturally and contextually appropriate solutions to local problems.

Action research became a formal strategy for inquiry into education as early as 1946, when it was taken up and advocated in the work of the Horace Mann-Lincoln Institute at Teachers College, Columbia University. It fell into decline in education as positivist forms of research won educators' interest. It was argued that research was no place for an amateur, teachers don't have time for research and it would detract from their teaching, the use of substitutes to replace teachers while they conducted research would lower the quality of students' education, and action research placed an extra financial burden on the school. Nevertheless, in the early 1970s, teachers and researchers began to question the applicability of traditional research methods to education. Now referred to as collaborative action research, action research in the schools focuses on curriculum, professional development, and organizational change.

Action Science. A 1970s descendent of Lewin's work with action research was action science, a highly specialized form of action research developed by Argyris (1993). Action science differs from action research in that the data are on previous actions taken by individuals, groups, or the organization as a whole. These data are then analyzed to determine whether or not the reasoning on which the action was based is problematic. Argyris suggests that people do not make mistakes on purpose. They would make the needed changes in their organizations without help if there were not some mental dilemma preventing rational action. In action science, individuals bring in cases of errors they have made in implementing change or solving an organizational problem. Individuals then meet in groups to examine what they were thinking and feeling but were not saying to see if a pattern of undiscussable issues needs addressing before change can be implemented. This analysis provides an examination of how people in problem situations reason. Over many years of work with individuals in organizations, Argyris has seen two dominant patterns of thought emerge: the desire to win or control the situation and the desire to be more open to learning. Most individuals hold both of these patterns; yet problematic cases tend to illustrate a control orientation. Action science is intended to aid individuals in becoming more comfortable using their learning orientation when in difficult circumstances.

Action Learning. Another important strain of action inquiry to spring up in the 1970s and 1980s has been directed at the improvement of professional practice. Found both in the field of management and education, these action technologies reject the knowledge of science or theory as the most important source informing practice and instead systematically implement Deweyan principles of experiential learning. In action learning as developed by Reg Revans (1982), for example, groups of professionals from different settings come together to help each other find solutions to their problems of practice. Typically, participants in an action learning group represent their own organizations so that learning is both a form of professional development and results in some form of organizational change. The process, which includes questioning the framing of the problem, collecting data, and trying solutions, rests on the power that strangers to a problem have to bring questions and perspectives different from those who "own" the problem, thus helping them see their situation in new ways.

Participatory Research and Popular Education. A vital stream among action technologies and one to which adult educators have particularly contributed is that of participatory research and popular education as practiced in both the United States and abroad. Frequently associated with the work of adult educators such as Freire (1974), Hall, Gillette, and Tandon (1982), and Fals-Borda and Ralman (1991), these action technologies are characterized by having members of oppressed, exploited, or marginalized groups talk about the problems they face and research how they are rooted in and related to the political and sociocultural structure of society. Members of the group then frequently take action to break down the mental and social patterns that hold their own oppression in place. Participatory research focuses this effort on a problem identified by the community that it wishes to solve. Popular education embeds this process of collective awareness-raising regarding the conditions of oppression in organized educational activities intended to impart specific basic skills such as literacy or numeracy.

Part of both of these action technologies is a critique of the monopoly on research and the production of knowledge by academicians who often work for their own professional enhancement and at the service of the dominant system rather than for the benefit of those they research. Central to both action technologies is the recognition that research is not value free, but is infused with moral and political interests, and the beliefs that we build our lives through our actions and society is the collection of these beliefs and actions.

Collaborative Inquiry. Finally, a nascent stream of action inquiry unites academics and practitioners who pursue understanding in some aspect of their practice or lives. This research differs from most forms of action inquiry in that it is intended explicitly to contribute to the formal knowledge base. However, it differs from traditional research in that it carries the value that knowledge cannot be "owned" and collaborative research requires a noncompetitive relationship among the co-researchers. Thus, collaborative inquiry has at its core an implicit intent to address these aspects of the academic research culture. Whereas much traditional research practice is blissfully non-self-reflective, the insight articulated in 1953 by Lewin that minority problems are in fact majority problems is translated in collaborative inquiry into the understanding that the practitioner problem of implementing theory into practice is in fact a scholar's problem.

Among the first to take a reflexive turn in academic research were feminist scholars who suggested that not only was traditional academic social research of limited use to practitioners, but it was also an oppressive imposition of a white male tradition on groups whose epistemology did not match this linear detached model (Reinharz, 1991). This has resulted in a form of participatory research by some university researchers that aims to find new, more democratic, and inclusive approaches to research. Such research focuses on a research problem that all members of the research group agree on, data including that gathered from outside the research group and through researcher personal experience, and a high degree of collaboration in the inquiry process.

Dimensions of Action Technologies

Although action technologies have a rich and varied history, they can be usefully compared along dimensions of similarity and difference. These dimensions are examined in the following sections.

Dimensions of Similarity. Action technologies are similar in four major dimensions. First is that their intended result is the construction of new knowledge on which new forms of action can be based. Although this description seems to say that knowledge precedes action, in fact the action-research cycle typically includes a cyclical process in which our action contributes to the knowledge we build, and the knowledge we build alters our action.

The second dimension is that those members who permanently work or reside in a particular context should be central to the research process. This theme reflects the observation that social science research or institutional knowledge imposed on an individual or group from above or from outside is often inappropriate, ineffective, and ill-received. It also reflects the belief that practitioners, community members, and workers who must act in the context are in a better position to explore their existing patterns of thought and practice than are social scientists from the outside.

The third dimension is that the data used in the research process are systematically collected and come from the experience of the participants. The element of systematicity removes action technologies from the realm of simple reflective practice or experiential learning and places them solidly in a broadly defined field of research. The research question is formulated, the research process is carefully designed, data collection and analysis are carried out, conclusions are drawn, and new questions are formulated by the co-researchers. Thus, the learning process is formalized and systematized as an organized research process, drawing on the experiences and methodologies of others who have used similar methodologies.

The final theme is that all of these action technologies are focused on change. Action is studied, probed, and pondered in order to make improvements in professional practice, organizational outcomes, or social democracy.

Dimensions of Difference. Action technologies differ along several important dimensions, as well. One of the most important is the political dimension. Many writers have distinguished between whether the technology is intended to improve the effectiveness of an institution or improve the conditions of the co-researchers. In other words, is the technology used as a tool of management or as a method for promoting liberation and justice among the co-researchers? The former usually occurs in the workplace, and the latter in a community setting. This distinction has become common in discussions about action technologies, casting one type of action inquiry as a handmaiden of industry, and another type as an agent of freedom for the oppressed. Put bluntly, the question is whose interests does the action technology serve? This question is further compounded by the fact that all of the action technologies discussed in this book are potentially disruptive of existing power relationships. Practitioners who want to control their own practice—teachers, for example—are unlikely to comply with hierarchically imposed standardized curriculums. Workers who want to control their own work may find that the problems that are reducing efficiency rest ultimately with management and management systems rather than with faulty micro-level work systems. Community members may conclude that the persistent blocks to their equal access to resources or to economic advancement rest with public policy. These conclusions are potentially disruptive to the existing social order and lend a paradoxical quality to action technologies in that in many instances the research must be condoned and funded by the very groups or individuals whose privilege in the social order is at stake.

However, this polarized view of the oppressed and the oppressors increasingly masks a more complex social reality. As industrialized nations shift from production to information-oriented societies, the gap between the rich and the poor seems to be widening and the size of the middle-class diminishing. This makes the social position of the marginalized in industrialized countries and the poor in Third World nations more analogous to that of the middle-class in this country. Increasingly, we are coming to understand the lack of power the mass of people have over their own lives in industrialized societies. Reason captures the increasing relevance of action technologies to all social classes when he writes, "We need to learn how to take the value and spirit of inquiry into economic, political, personal, and spiritual life as a counterweight to narrow-mindedness, authoritarianism, and chauvinism. We need participative action research as one way to re-invent our society and democracy in the face of political, economic, and maybe most importantly environmental crises" (Reason, 1993, p. 18).

A second dimension along which action technologies may differ is whether they work more as a social version of the scientific experimental method or as a form of critical reflection on the part of the researchers and co-researchers. The experimental scientific method has at its heart a reflection-action cycle by which a hypothesis is put forward, an action is taken to test it, and the results are used to add to and refine the knowledge accumulated. This is a functional perspective on knowledge. Action technologies practiced from this perspective are for the purpose of adjusting action to achieve a concrete objective that usually pertains to increasing efficiency as in projects intended to reduce the time it takes to manufacture a product or to combat social prejudice.

Action technologies from a more critical perspective aim at identifying dysfunctional patterns, critiquing them, and imagining alternative ways of thinking and acting. In a liberating mode, this has usually meant identifying ways in which the cultural stories of an oppressive system have been internalized by oppressed groups and classes without reflection. Once identified, these cultural stories can be transformed into objects to be observed and more authentic cultural stories given voice. Action technologies that incorporate critical reflection within a management context usually look for ways in which habitual patterns of thought and action interfere with a psychologically and socially healthy work environment.

A third dimension along which action technologies may differ is the degree to which the researcher and the co-researchers share power. Although all action strategies rely on data generated by the co-researchers, they do not all include the co-researchers in determining the problem to be researched, the analysis of data, and the writing up and publishing of conclusions.

A fourth dimension along which they may differ is how the knowledge generated is used. Research has traditionally had the intention of generating theory that was predictive and could be applied to multiple settings, provided they were similar enough. Action technologies on the other hand have focused on producing theory that could be used to solve local and frequently idiosyncratic problems. This has meant that action researchers have not typically contributed the knowledge they produce to the body of formal theory.

Recently, however, many have questioned the importance we have given to the generalizing of research findings. Observing that generalizations are of limited value in working with unique individuals and contexts, the search for universal laws has lost some of the appeal it has historically held for many researchers and practitioners. One way of describing this shift is to contrast research for the purpose of prediction with research for the purpose of learning. Research for the purpose of prediction holds the promise of control in that, by telling us what occurs in similar situations the majority of times, the probability is that if we act a particular way, we will get a particular result. Research for the purpose of learning makes no such promise. Rather than helping us "play the odds," research for learning helps us know more about ourselves and our work from reading about the experiences of others. Through learning about the experiences of others, we get ideas, new ways of thinking, a sense of the uniqueness of our own context, and a window into ourselves. Research for learning is research for humans who must find their own way through unique situations rather than ask experts for general advice. For managers, for example, it is not good enough that an action yield a particular result 82 percent of the time. They need that result just once, with the company they lead.

Although recent forms of action inquiry are more oriented toward learning for unique situations, some older forms of action inquiry attempted to generate generalizable knowledge using statistical methods. Nevertheless, historically much of action inquiry has generated knowledge that has remained within the context in which it was created. However, with the recent change in views about what kinds of knowledge are worthy of contribution to a formal knowledge base, it has become increasingly acceptable to contribute local knowledge generated by action research to journals and books. Similarly, action researchers have developed a considerable knowledge base about intervention or change theory, problem-framing and solving, organization development, and group or team learning and development. This in itself is an appropriate and significant contribution.

The Power of Practitioner-Researcher Collaboration

Action technologies possess a unique power in that they combine the skills and interests of both researchers and practitioners to create new knowledge. Practitioners, for example, are very sensitive to the relationship between researchers and the researched. They bring an insider's understanding to the community and organizational context. Similarly, they often have highly developed skills in establishing a climate of participation and honesty. These abilities assure that the research process works rather than aborts, and that the data gathered and decisions made are closely linked and useful to those actually in the context.

On the other hand, researchers bring with them a reflective and critical ability that helps break out of perspectives that have become dysfunctional. They are frequently skeptical about a problem as it is initially posed and resist early closure. They value multiple sources of data and are often knowledgeable about different methods of data collection and analysis. This assures that the process is systematic and generates a quality of knowledge not achievable in less formal problem-solving efforts.

The uniting of such diverse skills holds enormous promise for the production of both informal and formal knowledge. The potential for action technologies to address the challenges of rapid change, diverse populations, and diminishing natural resources in innovative ways is increased as researchers working with practitioners make their research more relevant and gain the tools to systematically and critically reflect on their own practice. The current questioning within the communities of researchers and practitioners seems to be heralding a change that allows inquiry and action to come together in a mutually productive fashion. Current forms of action technologies reflect the changes that are occurring as we confront both a crises in practice and a crises in the production of knowledge. In a fast-paced world, action technologies offer a tool of inquiry and learning that makes no pretense toward uncovering universal laws, but enables researchers and practitioners to continuously learn and develop new knowledge that is sensitive to changing and dynamic situations.

We live in a time of change. There often seem to be no models or traditions that can tell us what we should do in our lives or how we should act. Action technologies have always addressed the unpredictability of life and the situatedness of action and practice. Perhaps in response to this unpredictability, in recent years practitioners and researchers, alone and in collaboration, have developed new ways to develop useful knowledge. New kinds of action technologies have been developed to be used in unique situations to address unique problems. Action technologies are tools for individuals, organizations, and communities to learn their way through their problems. Using them most effectively often means trying an existing technology and then adapting it to specific needs and unique contexts.

Conclusion

This chapter has framed the issues that have led to a resurgence of interest in action technologies: a disillusionment with professional or scientific knowledge coupled with a reassertion of trust in practitioner knowledge; an increasing focus on more widespread development and use of knowledge; and changing conceptions of the relationship between power and knowledge. Many different approaches to action inquiry have evolved in response to these issues. The chapter has situated action technologies as an approach to change that enables individuals and organizations to bridge the gap between theory and practice and address the pressing problems of a quickly changing world.

References

Adams, F. *Unearthing Seeds of Fire.* Winston-Salem, N.C.: John F. Blair, 1975.
Argyris, C. *Knowledge for Action: A Guide to Overcoming Barriers to Organizational Change.* San Francisco: Jossey-Bass, 1993.
Corey, D. "Action Research to Improve School Practices." *Teachers College Record,* 1953.
Dewey, J. *Experience and Education.* New York: Collier, 1963. (Originally published 1938.)
Fals-Borda, O., and Ralman, M. A. *Action and Knowledge.* New York: Apex Press, 1991.
Forgacs, D. (ed.). *An Antonio Gramsci Reader.* New York: Schocken Books, 1988.
Freire, P. *Pedagogy of the Oppressed.* New York: Seabury Press, 1974.

Hall, B., Gillette, A., and Tandon, R. *Creating Knowledge: A Monopoly?* New Delhi, India: Society for Participatory Research in Asia, 1982.

Lewin, K. "Action Research and Minority Problems." *Journal of Social Issues,* 1946, 2.

Lindeman, E. C. *The Meaning of Adult Education.* Montreal: Harvest House, 1989. (Originally published 1961.)

Reason, P. "Sitting Between Appreciation and Disappointment: A Critique of the Special Education of Human Relations on Action Research." *Human Relations,* 1993, *46* (10), 1253.

Reinharz, S. *On Becoming a Social Scientist.* New Brunswick, N.J.: Transaction, 1991.

Revans, R. *The Origin and Growth of Action Learning.* Bickly, England: Chartwell-Bratt, 1982.

Trist, E., and others. *Organizational Choice.* London: Tavistock, 1963.

Whyte, W. F. (ed.). *Participatory Action Research.* Newbury Park, Calif.: Sage, 1991.

ANN BROOKS is assistant professor in the Adult Education and Human Resource Development Program, University of Texas at Austin, and a member of the Group for Collaborative Inquiry.

KAREN E. WATKINS is associate professor of adult education, University of Georgia, and former director of the graduate program in human resource development, University of Texas at Austin.

*Action Reflection Learning™ can help managers learn transforma-
tively, and because their learning takes place in teams that work on
real organizational problems, it can lead to systems change and organizational capacity building.*

Becoming Critically Reflective Through Action Reflection Learning™

Judy O'Neil, Victoria J. Marsick

Companies are trying to survive in a rapidly changing, turbulent environment. Managers are faced with external challenges—such as high technology, glob-alization, political and social reorganization—and internal challenges—Total Quality, reengineering, downsizing, flattening of the hierarchy, and participa-tive management, for example. In the past, training and education prepared managers for a more predictable world. To manage rapid change, today's man-agers need new competencies such as critical thinking, the ability to question the "way things are done around here," leadership skills, continuous learning capacity, the ability to help others and the organization learn, high performance teamwork, and skill in designing innovative solutions and processes.

New competencies cannot be imparted in traditional ways because prob-lems are so complex that one "best" solution cannot easily be advocated; man-agers must hone their judgment in deciding how to apply wisdom gained through experience in situations that demand answers tailored to the people and problems involved; and solutions are changing so quickly that they can-not easily be packaged and passed on to others before they themselves be-come obsolete.

As a result, many organizations are experimenting with new ways of devel-oping managers. In many of these experiments, learning strategies are moving outside of the classroom and into the work site. The rationale is that managers are more motivated to learn when confronting real issues, and the competen-cies they gain through this kind of learning better enable them to deal with the continually changing, complex problems the environment engenders.

This chapter describes an action technology—Action Reflection Learning™ (ARL), a variant of Action Learning (AL)—that illustrates this new approach.

The examples we use are drawn from management development in business, but ARL can be used in different settings with different types of learners. ARL's strengths are many, but the facet we focus on here is the way in which this strategy builds critical reflection in managers, and through them, in the culture of their companies.

We start by defining Action Reflection Learning™ and differentiating it from Action Learning. We describe its program design and examine its theoretical underpinnings in critical reflection. We then discuss examples from several different programs that illustrate the way in which ARL builds critical reflection that develops individuals and teams as they solve organizational problems. We conclude with a look at several factors to consider in choosing to implement ARL, given its focus on critically reflective learning.

History and Definition of Action Reflection Learning™

The name Action Reflection Learning™ has been coined to emphasize the role of reflection in Action Learning. Action Learning is often credited to an English physicist, Reg Revans, who was charged with responsibility for management development for the coal mines in the 1930s during a time of industrial crisis. Revans (1982) suggested that knowledge came from action rather than the study of books. Books hold programmed wisdom from the past (P learning), whereas managers need questioning insight (Q learning), which they can only develop by wrestling with live problems and subsequently reflecting upon results. Revans aimed at a synergy of mind and body, which is not imparted by an educator or expert but is gained more appropriately through the reinterpretation of the learner's own experience and existing knowledge (Pedler, 1991).

ARL does not differ in concept from the central thrust of AL, but it does differ in application. The latter has been widely interpreted and practiced, so much so that it is sometimes hard to determine what AL really looks like. In a recent article, for example, Froiland (1994) describes the following as Action Learning: outdoor adventure learning activities; "Gap Groups" in which AT&T employees help one another address performance gaps; GE's Workout! sessions in which concerned stakeholders gather in one room to analyze a process or problem and tender solutions which they are then commissioned to enact; and global leadership conferences at Whirlpool in which participants brainstormed a list of needed projects and formed teams subsequently sent off to tackle selected projects. Revans (1982) defines AL's essence as learning from and with peers while tackling real problems; as such, his definition might hold true for all of the above examples. However, it is difficult to determine the extent to which these examples promote learning through action and the extent to which they are simply good task forces or problem solving groups. ARL holds that there must be an equal emphasis on both learning and doing, and that people do not always know innately how to learn in this way from their experience. ARL is designed to maximize the creative tension that occurs when participants strike a balance between learning and doing. Measures are taken to ensure that learning is not simply presumed to occur along the way.

In this form of action technology, the paradigm of training becomes for-ever changed because "training" is actually working on a problem that has strategic importance to an organization. ARL's basic characteristics include the following (Marsick, Cederholm, Turner, and Pearson, 1992, p. 64):

Working in small groups to solve problems
Learning to learn and think critically
Building skills to meet the learning needs that emerge during a program
Developing a participant's own theory of management, leadership, or empow-erment—a theory that is tested against real world experience, as well as established tenets.

ARL is sometimes referred to as business-based management development. At the heart of its design is a combination of action—through project work on actual problems—and reflection—separate, specifically designed opportuni-ties to think about what took place.

The project forms a "laboratory" for experimentation. ARL teams work on projects that are chosen based on the following criteria:

Projects are complex, overarching, and often cross boundaries and functions.
Projects are real work, that is, a problem or challenge with no known solu-tion—not a puzzle with a known answer.
Projects are meaningful to each person involved in the program.
Solutions are those over which reasonable people can disagree.

Managers take action and think about the results, using the help of a team advisor and others on the team to see the situation in new ways. They learn from their experience as they work, taking time to reflect together about new insights into the problem and its solutions, their work together as a team, and their own learning patterns (Watkins and Marsick, 1993). Managers learn how to ask fresh questions, which is key to this type of learning. For example, rather than ask, "What is the solution to this problem?" they may ask, "Is this the right problem for us to be solving?" Also, instead of wondering, "Will this solution be acceptable to our company?" they may ask, "What's wrong with the norms of our company that we are wondering if our solution will be accept-able?" They try out new behavior and get feedback, and thus gain insight into similar problems back on their own jobs. Managers learn to act and reflect so they may learn, and they reflect on the learning so that they may act more effectively (O'Neil and DiBona, 1993).

Characteristically, managers reformulate their understanding of the prob-lems underlying the project, and the project itself, as they uncover assump-tions, misperceptions, norms, and expectations that are often hidden from themselves and others. One example of this reformulation process was an ARL group whose project assignment was to answer this question: "What should quality work be in the future and how should we measure it?" As a result of differences in background of the group members, the question moved from dealing with technical measurements, to consideration of software solutions, to the reformulated question of "What does the philosophy and vision of the company need to be for the nineties?"

ARL Program Design

A program designed for Volvo Truck Corporation by related agencies Management Institute, Lund, Sweden (MiL) and Institute for Leadership in International Management (LIM) provides some insight into the design of an ARL program (Management Institute, Lund, Sweden, and Institute for Leadership in International Management, 1993). This program was the third in a series. Care was taken to select projects that concern real, complex issues over which reasonable people disagree. Volvo Truck Corporation looked for corporate global projects with regional implications that held actual and strategic importance. They wanted projects that were demanding, innovative, achievement-oriented, with possibility for risk taking and a likelihood of a quantifiable payoff. The projects in this program centered on benchmarking, lead times, special vehicles, and powertrain components. Participants were given some choice in selecting the project on which they would work, but teams were designed to maximize differences in function, background, company experience, and perspective so that fresh questions could be asked. A critical feature of ARL is that no one on the team functions as an expert to which others will turn for advice, consciously or unconsciously. Reliance on experts often discourages "dumb questions" that give rise to new avenues of thinking.

Four week-long residential seminars were designed to launch the projects. These seminars served as a forum for issues that arose in project work and as a means to instill the new values and attitudes needed for a unified global business focus. Each seminar had a theme: the global perspective; the business perspective; the personal or professional and team perspective; or Volvo Truck Corporation's future leadership perspective. The seminars took place in March, May, September, and November. These seminars included both work on projects and short content segments. In addition, each group spent approximately twelve less structured days between seminars on project work (Volvo Truck Corporation, 1993).

The Volvo Truck Corporation design is typical of the kind of program which MiL has been creating in Europe for over ten years. Each of MiL's programs is typically designed for fifteen to twenty managers divided into smaller teams (sets) of three to four people each. Programs are sometimes designed for many companies, sometimes for one company, and sometimes for a group of companies that choose to work together as learning partners. These programs take more time than most "training" activities because participants work on real-life problems that do not get solved overnight. For example, programs may take twenty to forty person-days spread out over six to nine months in a "sandwich" format, that is, short activities (one-half day to five days each) scheduled in between regular work, along with flexibly-planned, less structured project work. LIM models its programs on MiL, but programs in the United States are more frequently offered within companies, perhaps because of proprietary interests. Internal programs are often used to launch major organizational initiatives, beginning with senior executives and moving down through middle management.

MiL programs typically have three parallel tracks: projects (experience and reflection seminars); workshops and seminars on issues that arise from project work, scheduled as appropriate; and discussion of back-home concerns that arise as participants reexamine concerns from their daily work in light of new learning. The art of ARL rests, in part, on the weaving together of these three strands into an integrated whole. Often a central theme is used to unify tracks, such as global leadership in the Volvo Truck Corporation program. A central feature of both MiL and LIM programs is a personal development component to help managers understand themselves better in relationship to the demands being placed on them by new work. The timing of this component is important: if scheduled too early, the managers have not yet received enough feedback through their project work, and thus, do not recognize its value; if scheduled too late, there is not enough time to try out new behaviors and attitudes based on self-insight gained in these activities.

MiL and LIM program designs are very dependent on the skills and abilities of the Project Team Advisors (PTAs), especially in the initial stages of the program. This feature differentiates ARL from AL, where facilitation may well be left to the skills of those in the group, or if provided, may not be as clearly focused on reflection to assist learning. PTAs in ARL help project teams learn the following:

How to frame and reframe the problem or challenge accurately, since complex issues are seldom what they first seem

How to identify, clarify, and test one's personal insights and "theories" about the problem or challenge

How to reflect on the way in which problems and challenges are formulated, tested, and solved

How to continually learn how to learn, both individually and when naturally interacting with others in groups and teams

How to use the issues that arise in project work to understand and manage similar issues that are faced back on the job.

By acting as a challenger, questioner, and mirror of the team's actions, the PTA helps participants dig below the surface and reflect on the values, expectations, norms, and beliefs that shape the way in which they understand the problem. Through this type of activity, the basis is laid for critical reflection.

Critical Reflection: Definition and Examples

Mezirow (1991) unpacks the meaning of the word "reflection," which is often used but undoubtedly with different meanings. Drawing on John Dewey, Mezirow points out that reflection involves attending to the grounds of one's beliefs and, by extension of some theorists, of one's feelings as they contribute to the validity of one's thinking. Dewey was interested in reflection as it related to problem solving, which is the focus of much workplace learning. Mezirow points out that Dewey did not differentiate types of reflection: that which focused on the nature of the problem itself, that which focused on the process of problem solving, and that which focused on the premises or presuppositions that lie at the foundation of one's definition of a situation. Mezirow does make these distinctions, and in doing so, points out that "The critique of premises or presuppositions pertains to problem *posing* as distinct from problem *solving*" (p. 105).

Problem posing involves raising questions that open up new dimensions of thinking about the situation, whereas in problem solving, a person often looks primarily at solutions without questioning whether or not the initial assessment of the situation is the only one, or the best one, that is possible. For example, during an ARL meeting facilitated by Marsick, one manager questioned whether or not others really agreed that they had been learning quite a lot in the session, or whether they simply fell into the trap of pretending they agreed. Managers were asked to go around the table to share what each felt he or she learned. This led to a discussion of the culture of their workplace with respect to telling the truth. Each manager had a story to tell about being truthful. This eventually led to an exploration of whether or not basic norms in the institution had changed, as evidenced by the way in which truth was rewarded or punished through budget cuts or appropriations, career boosts, and other tangible or intangible proof that truth was or was not valued. This kind of problem posing is quite typical of the discussion that occurs in ARL programs. As a result, the group's understanding of a problem frequently gets reframed.

Another example comes from an ARL group whose focus was employee satisfaction that began with an investigation of extrinsic rewards. An analysis of Total Quality and its links to employee satisfaction led to the awareness that meaningful work in a Quality culture might be a stronger motivator than extra pay or benefits. As this group explored the concept of a Quality culture, they realized that a key characteristic was respect. One indicator of a lack of respect was that employees were often interrupted, albeit with stated apologies, in the middle of phone calls or closed-door meetings by others who demanded immediate information or attention. Of course, the interrupters were likewise being pushed by their managers or clients. Such behavior did not feel respectful, nor did it result in high quality work because attention was diverted to multiple uncompleted tasks. Problem posing began with extrinsic rewards, moved to meaningful work, and ended with the way in which the company could create a culture of respect.

Mezirow calls reflection on basic premises that underlie thinking by the name of "critical reflection" (p. 105) and points out that, although it takes place less frequently than reflection on the content or processes of problem solving, critical reflection has the potential to transform thinking because it is directed at our basic understanding of the experiences that we have. In premise reflection, people recognize that their perceptions may be flawed because they are filtered through uncritically accepted views, beliefs, attitudes, and feelings inherited from one's family, school, and society. Such flawed perceptions often distort one's understanding of problems and situations. Managers point out that taking time to reflect in even a surface fashion is highly powerful because they have a natural predilection to action that is reinforced by the nature of their work—putting out fires and solving problems quickly—and by a perception of urgency because of shortened product cycles and the real threat of extinction in the marketplace. Critical reflection is even more powerful because attention is directed to the root of the problem. Why spend time moving the deck chairs if the Titanic is sinking?

There are many strategies available to encourage critical reflection, a number of which are described in Mezirow and Associates (1990). ARL is one such strategy; it promotes critical reflection in several ways. First, project teams are designed so that managers will ask questions of one another that don't normally get asked because of the diverse perspectives that they bring to the situation. Managers are often truly surprised when they learn of the different interpretations others hold of a common experience. They often proceed on the assumption that everyone holds the same understanding as they do, and as a result, each is attempting to solve a very different problem even though everyone uses the same vocabulary. Second, the project team advisor (PTA) creates a climate that encourages dialogue, critique, and reflection by stopping the action periodically in order to help participants dig below the surface of their comments and behavior—with respect to the question under discussion, the dynamics of the group, or individual statements and actions. Third, the PTA often introduces tools and methods, in a just-in-time learning format, that can help to support and encourage critical reflection. For example, after a group has begun work on their project, group members often encounter difficulties in the process due to the fact that they are not all working with the same set of shared assumptions. Once the group has reached this juncture, the PTA will intervene with some just-in-time learning in which he or she explains the process, and value, of surfacing and discussing participants' assumptions about their project work. Fourth, ARL promotes real-time feedback from the PTA and peers about events that arise in the group. One way in which this is done is through fishbowls in which PTAs discuss observations, hunches, and perceptions in a circle in the center of the remaining participants, followed by dialogue with participants to check out viewpoints and test the validity of their observations. Real-time feedback makes discussable the many perceptions that people hold, but seldom disclose, and yet act upon. This helps managers begin to reflect on premises that shape the way they think about problems and solve them. Fifth, ARL encourages action to test out individual and collective beliefs, hunches, and solutions. The outcome of a project is not typically an extensive report that will sit on shelves. For example, a project team might conduct focus groups, implement a customer opinion survey, pilot test a solution, or create and screen a video to dramatically illustrate some aspect of the problem in order to catalyze discussion.

Watkins and Marsick (1993) use the concepts of reflection and critical reflection to develop a model of continuous learning that builds upon the problem-solving cycle discussed by John Dewey and later by Argyris and Schön (1974) in their work on action science. The model consists of concentric inner and outer circles that represent layers of learning. In the middle of the circle are the challenges one experiences at work. The inner circle represents the simple steps of the problem-solving cycle: experience the problem or challenge, examine alternative solutions, produce the solution, and plan next steps. A level of learning is attainable by reflecting on the nature of the problem and on the problem-solving process itself that enables a person to (1) see the challenge as a learning opportunity; (2) open him or herself to a variety of ways of thinking about solutions; (3) identify what is needed and learn about what one does not know to implement the solution; and then (4) subject the results to a rigorous examination to learn from the experience for similar future challenges.

There is also a deeper level of learning that is attainable by reflecting on the premises that underlie one's understanding at each step in this cycle. At the first step, one can dig below the surface to examine the beliefs, feelings, and past experiences through which one subconsciously filters an encounter with a new situation. This conscious level of awareness helps one to avoid habitual responses and remain open to a fresh assessment of what will be encountered. However, to do so requires some way of breaking out of our usual frame of reference. We can be helped to do so in many ways, for example, through the questions of people unlike ourselves or the surprise we experience in situations unfamiliar to us. At the second step, one can delve more deeply into the context in which the problem is embedded so that new alternatives can be identified. What assumptions do we make about what we can and cannot do, what will or will not be supported, who will react in what ways? Are there steps that we can take to test our assumptions before automatically acting upon limiting beliefs? At the third step, one can stop and think while implementing a solution in order to see the gaps that exist between what we think we do (our espoused theory) and what we actually do (our theory-in-use). We all have blind spots that prevent us from being effective, yet others may be unwilling or unable to give us the feedback we need to see these blind spots or we may be unwilling to hear feedback when given. Moreover, Argyris (Argyris and Schön, 1974) maintains that we are often highly skilled at our incompetence, and therefore, cannot easily unlearn years of practice even when we want to act in new ways. Finally, at step four, we can look for the unintended consequences along with the intended ones. To do so often requires distancing ourselves from what we expected to see and speaking to those who hold opposing views.

An illustration of this cycle comes from a program that O'Neil managed. Personal development is an integral part of the MiL and LIM program designs. In one such program, a component of that personal development dealt with the individual taking responsibility for, and expressing, his or her thoughts, feelings, and wants. A behavior that helped to demonstrate that ownership was the use of "I" language (Short, 1991). The process one of the teams went through during the personal development part of their program also illustrates the continuous learning cycle. This team came to understand that behavior, which they and their organization had supported, produced counter-productive, time-wasting results.

From the outset, there was resistance from the team regarding the appropriateness of using "I" instead of "we" in their discussions within the team. They thought that using "we," as was the custom in the organization, better demonstrated support of the team environment in which they worked. During the ensuing discussions, the PTA asked if it was really possible to have a "we" until the voices of the "I's" that made up that "we" were known. This question helped the team to start to *reframe* their roles as team members in both the ARL program and back on their job. After the opportunity to practice this new behavior during the ARL program, team members agreed that they would try to use the behavior back on the job. There continued to be concern about others' reactions to this perceived non-team behavior, so the participants agreed that they would choose opportunities in which they felt a degree of safety.

At the next ARL session, with the PTA's guidance, the team spent time reflecting on, and discussing, the results of their new behavior. They realized that *the assumptions* they had held about negative reactions and lack of support from others were unfounded. After some initial reactions of surprise and some discomfort, other members of the organization expressed that they thought the new behavior helped to clarify the work and make the teams more productive. To further assist the ARL team with their learning, the PTA also asked them to reflect on questions that dealt with their previous behavior in team meetings, and the results of that behavior. As a result of that reflection, combined with the earlier discussion on their current behavior, the team was able to see that there had been a *mismatch between their theory-in-use and their espoused theory.* They espoused wanting to be members of productive, supportive teams, yet their behavior engendered confusion and lack of ownership and support. Some of the *unintended consequences* they discovered were wasted time due to lack of clarity, public support and private disagreement, and team members who were uncommitted to decisions to which they felt they had never agreed.

This next example illustrates an ARL team in which some of the members used critical reflection to help break through a mindset that said that, in order for them to be successful, they had to "be told" exactly what the organization expected of them. This team had a very slow start in their work because they felt they needed to get greater clarity from the client about their project. During a reflection stop in this time period, the PTA asked them to think about why they were not progressing with their work. The team members' response was that they could not proceed with their work until their client was clearer with expectations about the project. At this point, one of the team members asked "why" and changed the way the team looked at their lack of progress.

The ensuing discussion brought to light that some team members were unprepared to deal with ambiguous situations. Although the organization espoused an environment that supported risk taking, the reality, as perceived by those team members, was that of punishment for straying from the status quo. This disclosure prompted other team members to begin to examine the unintended consequences of this theory-in-use. Not only was it stopping progress on their ARL project, but they realized that it would hinder the organization in finding new and innovative solutions and initiatives. As a result of this critical reflection, these team members recognized that they needed to explicitly encourage, acknowledge, and reward risk taking in their peers and subordinates.

Factors to Consider in Choosing ARL

The continuous learning cycle that we describe here is the basis of several of the action technologies that embody critical reflection (O'Neil, 1992). In ARL, the focus is first and foremost on the development and learning of participants. This focus differentiates ARL groups from task or problem-solving groups. However, tangible gains such as money saved or as innovative solutions to difficult challenges frequently result from project work, in part because the emphasis on learning encourages new insights as projects are reframed and seen in fresh perspective. In selecting ARL, an adult educator would be interested in a task-based intervention that involves a group of people in a real project of relevance to them all that could also be used as a springboard for learning about themselves, the learning process, team work, and organizational change.

Table 2.1 lists some of the factors that MiL and LIM have found to be key principles for ARL interventions. Some of these probably hold true for any change intervention. Others are unique to ARL, in part because of the critically reflective dimension of these programs, in part because ARL is aimed at systems change as well as individual development. Critically reflective managers are likely to challenge norms, which companies may not welcome, even if they have said that they desire such challenge, as Brooks (1989) found in her research. Adult educators who work with ARL programs—whether internal managers, human resources staff, or consultants to the organization—must be prepared to stand firm when an ARL program "makes waves." "Making waves" is, in a sense, its purpose. An ARL project group is a laboratory for larger-system change, which cannot take place without such challenges.

An example comes from a MiL project with a consumer cooperative that focused upon decentralization of authority to retail units. "Headquarters had framed the problem in terms of a lack of courage on the part of retail store owners, but the store owners said that. . . . (mandated procedures, for example, budgets and regulations) did not allow them to take full control" (Marsick and Watkins, 1990, p. 62). The project group designed an experiment in which they stopped following mandated procedures that they believed were not cost-effective. They also ordered products that Headquarters frowned upon—for

Table 2.1. Selected Principles for
Action Reflection Learning™ Interventions

"Nutrients" That Support Success	*"Killers" That Contribute to Failure*
Top leadership acts in accordance with the vision and values of program.	Top management is not committed.
The power people structure, learn, and change.	The intervention is not interrelated with "the system."
The environment is one of trust, not one of fear.	Risks and mistakes are not tolerated.
The intervention engages participants' hearts, heads, and guts.	There is inconsistent, part-time participation.
The intervention supports authentic behavior in line with participants' values and beliefs.	The intervention is seen as a passing fad; that is, as "this too shall pass."
The program maximizes and respects diversity of all kinds through the mix of participants.	People who do not conform to the "right" corporate image are excluded.
Projects are built around real tasks of importance to the organization.	Projects are not seen as important to the business.
Facilitation is vital to the process.	The culture does not tolerate feedback.
A sponsor or champion is vital to the process.	Champions are not intrinsically motivated or are displaced.
The design team and participants are clear about the purpose of the intervention.	The intervention is seen as "stuff," separate events, not steps in a process, not strategically linked.
The company expects a curve in excitement, learning, and support.	Key players do not take the time to reflect, evaluate, redesign, renew.

Source: © 1993 by Institute for Leadership for International Management, Limited.

example, a brand of beer that was popular with consumers but produced by a competitor. Headquarters was distressed by the newly practiced autonomy of the store owners. The PTA helped the project group and Headquarters to examine the "waves" created and to see the gap that had to be closed between the perceived and actual intentions of Headquarters' framing of the problem.

The "waves" can come from individual action as well. At the start of any ARL intervention, there is a core of participants who begin to pave the way for those who will follow. These individuals sometimes take great personal risk as they begin to push against the system. A participant of one such team described a meeting in which she spoke out about her disagreement regarding an issue. The unspoken norms in the organization were to never disagree in an open forum. Her manager later confided in her that he felt the same way, but felt that he simply couldn't have said it. Her action at the meeting, small though it seems, helped to begin the ripples that eventually became waves. Neither the learning, nor the behavior change that can result from that learning, can take place if the environment is not perceived as a place that will be supportive.

As discussed earlier, an important differentiation of ARL is the balance between learning and doing. The doing side of the equation gets played out in the selection of the project work. In an ARL team that was part of a program O'Neil managed, the commitment of some members of a project team was negatively impacted when they perceived the project their group was working on was not of sufficient importance to the organization. The ARL program manager, and the PTA working with the team, spoke with the client about the concerns being voiced. The client responded with written and verbal support and assurance. Some of the doubts remained, however, and impacted the level of success achieved by the team. ARL works best when the client and organization understand the value that learning from "real," critical work provides to both participants and the organization, and are able to effectively relay their commitment to the projects to the participants.

Conclusion

ARL is an action technology that creates impact at many levels—the individual level, the team level, and the organizational level. At the individual level, it helps build competencies that enable business managers, and leaders in other settings, to address and solve complex problems in ambiguous environments. These individuals learn how to learn from the work in which they are involved on a daily basis and create their own management theories to deal with their changing worlds. At the team level, ARL provides competencies that enable individuals to effectively work in teams as both leader and member; competencies like the art of dialogue and the ability to provide constructive, meaningful feedback. At the organizational level, ARL teams solve strategic business problems, and through the competencies that participants gain at the individual and team level, they can positively change and shape their organizations. Although not always, companies often achieve significant gains to their bottom line as a result of ARL project team work. For example, one of the MiL's client organizations uses ARL as its primary management development tool and funds the entire management development budget from project results.

Even more significant gains are realized when critical reflection is involved. As we have shown, individuals learn how to surface, examine, and question the beliefs and assumptions that influence their actions and decisions. They learn to value the power of reflection on action in order to learn and shape future actions. They recognize that in their constantly changing, complex environment, it is no longer possible to know all the answers, but ARL helps them to learn to ask the right questions.

As a member of a team, through critical reflection, the ARL participant learns that other individuals may hold different assumptions and beliefs. This knowledge creates an awareness of the power of that diversity, and ARL provides the team with the competencies to help ensure these diverse opinions are raised and appreciated. At an organizational level, critical reflection in ARL provides the competencies to question and begin to effect changes in organizational norms. It provides participants with skills to compare actual behavior in their organizations against professed organizational norms, recognize when discrepancies exist, and take action to try to rectify the situation. Critical reflection helps to begin changes in organizational culture.

ARL's main focus early in an initiative is at the individual and team level. At these levels, individuals, and the teams in which they participate, are helped to gain the new competencies needed for their new environments. In addition, we believe that as ARL initiatives continue to mature, we can expect to see even greater impact at the organizational level.

References

Argyris, C., and Schön, D. *Theory in Practice: Increasing Professional Effectiveness.* San Francisco: Jossey-Bass, 1974.

Brooks, A. K. "Critically Reflective Learning Within a Corporate Context." Unpublished doctoral dissertation, Department of Higher and Adult Education, Teachers College, Columbia University, 1989.

Froiland, P. "Action Learning: Taming Real Problems in Real Time." *Training,* 1994, *31* (1), 27–34.

Management Institute, Lund, and Institute for Leadership in International Management. *Volvo Truck Management Program, VTM 3.* Program brochure. Lund, Sweden: Management Institute, Lund, and Institute for Leadership in International Management, 1993.

Marsick, V., Cederholm, L., Turner, E., and Pearson, E. "Action-Reflection Learning." *Training and Development,* 1992, *46* (8), 63–66.

Marsick, V. J., and Watkins, K. *Informal and Incidental Learning in the Workplace.* New York: Routledge, 1990.

Mezirow, J. *Transformative Dimensions of Adult Learning.* San Francisco: Jossey-Bass, 1991.

Mezirow, J., and Associates. *Fostering Critical Reflection in Adulthood: A Guide to Transformative and Emancipatory Learning.* San Francisco: Jossey-Bass, 1990.

O'Neil, J. *Combining Action Science with Action Reflection Learning.* Unpublished manuscript, Teachers College, Columbia University, 1992.

O'Neil, J., and DiBona, M. *Quality, the Learning Organization and AT&T.* Paper presented at the National Society for Performance and Instruction conference, Chicago, Apr. 1993.

Pedler, M. (ed.). *Action Learning in Practice.* (2nd ed.) Alsdershot, England: Gower, 1991.

Revans, R. *The Origin and Growth of Action Learning.* Bickly, England: Chartwell-Bratt, 1982.

Short, R. *A Special Kind of Leadership: The Key to Learning Organizations.* Seattle: The Leadership Group, 1991.

Volvo Truck Corporation. *VTM Newsletter,* no. 4 (December). Göteborg, Sweden: AB Volvo, 1993.

Watkins, K. E., and Marsick, V. J. *Sculpting the Learning Organization: Lessons in the Art and Science of Systemic Change.* San Francisco: Jossey-Bass, 1993.

JUDY O'NEIL is a doctoral candidate at Teachers College, Columbia University; adjunct professor of adult education; and an associate of the Institute for Leadership in International Management.

VICTORIA J. MARSICK is associate professor of adult and continuing education and chair, Department of Higher and Adult Education, Teachers College, Columbia University, and a founding member of the Institute for Leadership in International Management.

This chapter describes a Scandinavian form of action research that highlights co-researcher participation in design and decision making. This is a radical departure from traditional researcher-controlled research design and knowledge dissemination.

Democratizing Action Research at Work: A Scandinavian Model

Max Elden, Reidar Gjersvik

Programmatic action research (AR) aimed at democratizing working life in Norway began over three decades ago in the early 1960s, and with subsequent developments in Sweden and Denmark we can see the outlines of a Scandinavian model of action research. Originally the model was built on basic elements of action research as it was known in the United States. But it also incorporated other elements that reflect the focus on democratization, working life, and the Scandinavian context. Furthermore, in the last thirty years it has evolved substantially into something quite different from what it was in the early 1960s. While there was substantial similarity between the original model of action research in Norway and what is more generally known as action research, the new Scandinavian approach to democratizing action research at work has lead to new research roles and methods.

The Scandinavian approach of "democratizing action research" at work cuts two ways. First, it explicitly and publicly aims at democratizing work life. In contrast to the United States where work life improvements are generated primarily from short-term profit motives, in Norway action research has directly supported and contributed to laws and national policies aimed at democratizing working life. Second, and more important for our theme, for action research to have a democratizing effect, the research process itself may have to be democratized. If the objective is to empower people at work, the way action research is done may be as important as whatever substantive findings are produced.

To explore these ideas, we must first clarify what we mean by action research and how it was practiced in the Norwegian Industrial Democracy Program (NIDP) in the 1960s. Despite the success of the NIDP's first four field experiments, little locally generated, self-sustaining organizational democratization was occurring in Norway by the beginning of the 1970s. One of the strategies for breaking out of this lack of local diffusion was to rethink the action research process itself.

To give us a basis of comparison between the earlier form of AR and what had begun to develop by the early 1980s (Elden, 1979a, 1979b) and is still evolving (Elden and Chisholm, 1993), we describe in the next section a basic model of action research and how it was applied in the initial industrial democracy AR field experiments in Norway in the 1960s. We then describe a contemporary action research project in Norway that illustrates new action research practices and methods for the 1990s. Finally, we summarize the key elements of the new but still emerging Scandinavian action research model and relate it to similar developments in action research in the United States.

The Basic AR Model in the Early Norwegian Industrial Democracy Program

Comparing early discussions of action research such as Rapoport (1970) with reports of recent projects (Goode and Bartunek, 1990; Sommer, 1990) and reviews of the field (Peters and Robinson, 1984; Shani and Pasmore, 1985) reveals a high degree of consensus about what action research is and what constitutes its basic elements. Lewin (1946) and most subsequent writers have conceived of AR as a cyclical inquiry process that involves diagnosing a problem situation, planning action steps, implementing, and evaluating outcomes. Evaluation leads to diagnosing the situation anew based on learnings from the previous cycle. In short, action research aims at producing new knowledge that contributes both to practical solutions to immediate problems and to general knowledge.

The process of doing action research can be divided any number of ways. For our purposes five elements provide a useful model for describing the original action research field studies in Norway and contrasting them with current projects in order to identify the special characteristics of a contemporary "Scandinavian Model" of action research (Elden and Chisholm, 1993).

Purposes and Value Choice. In aiming to solve practical problems, action research necessarily takes a values position. Action researchers, rather than being "value neutral," select problems to study which they hope contribute to both general knowledge and practical solutions based on democratic, humanistic values. An action researcher has some vision of how society or organizations could be improved and uses the research process to help bring this desired future state into existence. Action research is change-oriented and seeks explicitly and directly to bring about change that has positive social value, such as healthy communities and democratic organizations.

Contextual Focus. A consequence of dealing with real world problems in a practical way is that action research is "context-bound" inquiry (Susman and Evered, 1978). Since problems are at least initially dependent on how they are defined by system members who experience them, action research is inter-disciplinary and "practice-theory" rather than theory-practice oriented. Problem definition is not limited to the concepts, theories, and epistemology of a particular discipline, but is grounded in the participants' definition of the context. The focus is on affecting the participants' way of understanding why they do what they do—what *their* "theory" is behind their practice—as a basis of developing a new, more effective "practice-theory." In the basic action research model in the context of working life, this inquiry occurs within a single unit or on one level of a system such as a work group, a department, or an organization usually within a relatively short time frame (a year or less).

Change-Based Data and Sense Making. In conducting research, the action researcher engages in a form of scientific inquiry and must follow the basic rules of the social sciences to support conclusions. Since action research is change-oriented, it requires data that help track the consequences of intended changes. So, action research must have data collected systematically over time. The core of the research process derives from interpreting and making sense from these data. From a research design perspective, an action research project in the basic AR model is like a field experiment. For example, in the classical AR projects by Coch and French (1948) or Pasmore and Friedlander (1982), the researchers formulated the research design, carried out the experiment or study, interpreted the data it generated, related findings to new theory, and reported results to the scientific community. In short, the researcher in the basic action research model acts as much as possible like a normal scientist. The researcher is the sole proprietor of the scientific aspects of the inquiry, the expert in charge of change and sense-making.

Participation in the Research Process. Action research would be impossible without some form of participation. Since action research focuses on problems of both practical and theoretical importance, it requires those who experience or "own" the real-world problem to be actively involved with the researcher at least in specifying the problem and sanctioning the search for solutions. This dependence on subjects requires feedback to and active interaction with them at least in the beginning and in the action phases of the research process. Collaboration also supports and encourages the ongoing cyclical and emergent nature of the action research process. System members, who would be passive subjects in traditional forms of research, must actively support the research process in action research. At least, they must participate as sponsors; at most, they can be part-time research assistants in sanctioning the research, helping define problems to which it should be addressed, and validating the researcher's findings.

Knowledge Diffusion. The diffusion of knowledge is essential to the scientific enterprise. Both normal science and the basic model of action research assume that a good solution to the chosen problem will spread by force of the value it adds to our general store of knowledge. Both involve relating the topic to existing literature in terms of where the theory-relevant part of the problem arose and writing up the results according to the canons of accepted social science practice. Susman and Evered (1978) identify specifying learning (identifying general findings) as a final stage of the action research process. This is typically the job of the researcher with little participation of system members.

The Norwegian Industrial Democracy Program

The Norwegian Industrial Democracy Program (NIDP) that started in the early 1960s was a good example of this five-step model. The NIDP is much too large and complex to analyze fully here. Fortunately, it has been fully documented in English (Elden, 1979b; Emery and Thorsrud, 1976). We provide a thumbnail sketch as a basis for describing the NIDP in terms of the five elements of our basic model of action research.

A tripartite committee of representatives from national unions, employers, and the government agreed in the early 1960s to sponsor research into restructuring work organization in Norwegian industry from a command and control to a self-managing paradigm. Today the idea of designing organizations based on self-managed work teams hardly seems revolutionary, but thirty years ago it was virtually unheard of as a principle upon which to base organization design and management. Although studies by the Tavistock Institute in British coal mines in the 1950s demonstrated the viability of "autonomous work groups" (Trist and others, 1963), there was no methodology for creating such forms of work organization in other industries. One of the most enduring accomplishments of the NIDP was to develop a viable methodology, "socio-technical systems," for analyzing and redesigning work organization.

The research team completed four action research field experiments during the last half of the 1960s at four different companies selected to represent leading Norwegian industries. In each project, a team of researchers did a socio-technical systems analysis, redesigned work organization accordingly, tracked the resulting effects, and wrote a substantial report. This meant that in each project it took more than a single researcher at least 12–18 months to do the research work. In the second phase of the NIDP, similar projects were successfully completed in various types of workplaces outside of the industrial sector (such as schools, shipping, medical supply, banking, government) in a much shorter period (typically three to six months). In each project, representatives from the local union and management joined with researchers to form a steering committee to oversee the project. However, in accord with the basic model of action research, the researchers were still in charge of the research. The findings repeatedly demonstrated the practical viability of what the Tavistock researchers termed "organizational choice" (Trist and others, 1963). In other words, it was feasible to organize production along self-management lines rather than the traditional top-down, command and control paradigm.

The NIDP is clearly a good example of action research. It aimed at solving a practical problem (restructuring work organization) by using a scientific approach such as field experiments and socio-technical systems concepts that also produced more general knowledge including theories of organization analysis, design, and democratization (Emery and Thorsrud, 1976; Elden 1979b, 1986). It can easily be described in terms of our five action research characteristics:

Purposes and value choice. The project was clearly values-driven in seeking to extend democracy in working life. Indeed there was a vision and a larger design aimed at democratizing society by starting with work organization (Elden, 1981a). The key was to install more democratic forms of work organization in leading segments of industry so that self-managed organization forms would then spread to all workplaces.

Contextual focus. The focus, fundamental "reengineering" of the organization and management of work, was a real-world topic. Researchers were heavily dependent on government, industry, and trade unions for project funding and sanctioning. The problem was cross-disciplinary and the research context defined. Its definition was shaped by stakeholder representatives, not just researcher or disciplinary-oriented categories.

Change-based data and sense making. Data were collected over time in a field study research design for which the researchers were responsible. The researchers collected data, analyzed it, and made conclusions; they did the research.

Participation in the research process. Stakeholder representatives on several levels participated in the national program. On the national level representatives of the major coalitions in public policy making participated by sanctioning and funding the project. On the level of individual projects, representatives of labor and management helped to define the specific organizational unit to be studied and provided initial feedback on draft research reports.

Knowledge diffusion. This was in its time the largest, most ambitious, and costliest action research program on record. It led to two work research institutes in Norway being established and a very rich documentation of a variety of projects (Elden, 1979b, 1983, 1986). The diffusion was not limited just to the world of ideas or formal field experiments. In the 1970s, these ideas spread to Sweden where they even impacted Volvo's assembly-line thinking. Today, of course, American car manufacturing is making well-known efforts along the same lines, and "reengineering" organizations by implementing self-managed work teams and the like has become more a consulting or organization development process than action research.

In summary, the NIDP as conceived and implemented in Norway in the 1960s was a good example of the basic model of action research that had been known from the 1940s. But it was more than that. The model in Norway had from the beginning explicit political goals and a strategy that involved national political sponsorship that could leverage workplace democratization into democratizing social change in the country as a whole (Emery and Thorsrud, 1976; Elden, 1981a).

The NIDP clearly was an action research program that aimed at making a difference—scientifically, practically, and politically. It made impressive advances in the 1960s when the first wave of four successful field experiments in key industrial sites was followed by similar projects in a variety of other types of workplaces including hotels, banks, schools, and the Norwegian merchant marine (Elden, 1979b). Nevertheless, by the early 1970s it was clear in Norway that the natural diffusion process essential for the overall political change strategy had stalled. Despite the positive results of the field study experiments, there was no self-sustaining local-level initiative available such as a model to help others change their own organization in the direction of increased democracy at work. Successful experiments did not even spread to other units within the same company. There were a variety of possible explanations. One was that an expressly political intervention would not diffuse in a market economy where there was no apparent economic incentive for radical organizational redesign. Another possible explanation for the "encapsulation" was politics and ideological differences. While no one disagreed with the idea of democracy in work life, representatives of the two major political groups disagreed about how to achieve it. The trade unions wanted to approach industrial democracy primarily by having union representatives on company boards. Representatives of the employers confederation opposed this and favored more participatory management on the workplace level.

Researchers, of course, had little control over any of this. What they could affect was the way action research was organized and managed. This led to starting up what proved to be a very significant new line of thinking in how to do action research. The AR model at the time was that of the research expert being in charge of the research process—the researcher was the "expert in charge of change" (Elden, 1981b).

The problem from this perspective was that if democratization depended on research done only by researchers and there were thousands and thousands of workplaces, you would never train enough AR-change experts. But even if one could overcome this limitation, an expert-based model seemed inconsistent with people learning how to study and change their own organization so that they could become empowered to change their organization in the future. The goal of democratizing work by people studying and changing their own organization conflicted with the way the action research process in the NIDP was organized and managed. A search began in the early 1970s at the Work Research Institute in Oslo for another model of AR that did not depend on unilateral and complete researcher control of the action research process. The results of this search after more than three decades are still evident in the many AR projects we find in Scandinavia today.

Examples of Scandinavian Action Research Today

There are a large number of action research projects in Scandinavian working life today (Davies, Naschold, and Pritchard, 1993; Engelstad and Gustavsen, 1993; Gjersvik, 1993; Gustavsen, 1992; Goranzon, 1991; Levin, 1993; Skule and Levin, 1993). We have selected a contemporary Norwegian AR project to illustrate how AR in Scandinavia in the 1990s relates to the earlier AR traditions. The project at Elkem Fiskaa (Aslaksen, 1991; Davies, Naschold, and Pritchard, 1993) demonstrates distinctive features of contemporary Scandinavian action research and helps us compare the model of action research at work in Scandinavia today versus 30 years ago.

Elkem Fiskaa Verk (Aslaksen, 1991), a silicon smelting plant, is part of the Elkem Group and has completed a project in which new work organization has led to more flexibility, better use of workers' tacit knowledge resources in manufacturing, and more participation and job satisfaction among the workers. Estimated productivity gain from 1990 to 1993 is 20 percent (Davies, Naschold, and Pritchard, 1993). The project is still in progress, and is currently being adopted on a corporate level for use at other Elkem plants.

In 1989, the Confederation of Norwegian Electrochemical and Metallurgical Industries and the Union of Norwegian Chemical Industry Workers began an initiative to start joint labor-management business development programs within the chemical process industry. Elkem Fiskaa Verk expressed a desire to participate, and a researcher from the Norwegian Work Life Centre started working with the company and its local union. The project itself started in spring 1990 at a time when the market for silicon was shifting rapidly, and the Elkem Fiskaa management recognized that the survival of the organization depended on better use of resources.

The entire project focused on the production department of the smelting plant. A union-management coordinating council was created to head the process. They agreed that the project should be based on the broadest possible employee participation, and that the new operator roles should provide "considerably more latitude and responsibility" (Aslaksen, 1991, p. 3).

At the beginning of the project, the researcher, along with representatives of labor, management, the Norwegian Work Life Centre, and Elkem Fiskaa Verk, defined two primary research purposes. The first was to develop new and improved organizational models that could be generalized for the Norwegian chemical-processing industry as a whole. The second was to inquire into why, contrary to expectations, the added expertise built up in the 1980s by the industry in general and by operators in particular had not led to higher productivity or to the establishment of more skilled, interesting jobs (Aslaksen, 1991). Results of the project showed that if skills and competence are going to be turned into a competitive advantage for the process industries, training must be made a part of the strategic development of the company. Training, in other words, must be considered as an investment rather than a cost, and it needs to be done in conjunction with the development of new, more democratic and effective organizational forms and work roles.

The project was started through a "search conference" in which all involved groups participated. A "search conference" is a highly participative strategic planning methodology which provides, in the course of two to three well-structured days, a democratic way of building consensus around a direction and generating specific action projects in which participants and others start to bring the new strategic intent into practice (Weisbord 1993; Crombie,

1985; Gustavsen and Engelstad, 1986; Herbst, 1980; Paalshaugen, 1986). It builds on systems thinking by getting the whole organizational system and its support functions (or at least individuals representing each part) into one room for several intensive workshop days. The conference lasts for one and one-half to two days and takes participants through a process of building consensus about a common history, major challenges, desired futures, and necessary actions. Some 70 people (out of a total 120 at the entire plant) participated in the search conference in the production department at Elkem Fiskaa; half of these were operators, and all the other departments in the plant were also represented.

The search conference produced numerous strategic action task forces in which some 50 people participated. In order to keep the project visible in the organization, the coordinating council tried to set up task forces with different completion dates so that results would be produced continuously. All task forces included ordinary workers, frequently as task force leaders. "The goal was to promote personal development by teaching a new way of working together and building up the expertise required to assume greater individual responsibility on the job" (Aslaksen, 1991, p. 4). Obviously, the project emphasized creating a self-development capacity in the organization as much as implementing specific changes.

One important result of the action research project was changes in work organization and staffing. In the traditional arrangement the day shift is in charge of all maintenance and repairs, since that is when the mechanics in the technical department work. This led to occasional delays, little flexibility, and poor use of human resources and skills on the other shifts. In particular, training and skills development among operators was meaningless as long as the skills could not be applied in their work. Through multiskilling and changes in the shift arrangements, simple maintenance and repairs began to be done by all shifts. This made work more skilled and meaningful for the workers as well as improved flexibility, quality, and productivity in the silicon smelting process. The long-term plan is to staff every shift with multi-skilled "PEMA teams" (processing, electrical, mechanical, automation) qualified to handle the entire process, and to train "PEMA operators."

In terms of researcher role, the perceived neutrality of the researcher was critical. Her coming from the outside, but not being employed by management, was a critical factor in the Elkem Fiskaa project as this gave her credibility in the organization. In addition, the focus on the different understandings that different groups of participants held about their organization and their work situation, and the inclusion of these understandings in the change process, gave the project a truly co-generative content. By co-generative, we mean a participative research process in which both the researched ("insiders") and the researchers ("outsiders") collaborate in "co-creating 'local theory' that the participants test out by acting on it. Sensemaking and research content are no longer the exclusive domain of the researcher alone. The results can be fed back to improve the participants' own 'theory' and can further generate more general ('scientific') theory" (Elden and Levin, 1991, p. 129–130). This means that the researchers and the organizational members jointly manage and contribute to the actions and the research, including issues, content, data construction, reflection, and publishing. At Elkem Fiskaa, members of the joint union-management coordinating council, the search conferences, and the task force groups were all were very much in charge of the project and its associated research agenda. The researcher's role was to be an expert on research design and methods and to be responsible for the "scientific" aspects of the project such as formal publication, valid data, and empirically sound reports (Elden, 1981b). In addition, she had an important political and legitimating role, as commented above.

Updating the Scandinavian Model of Action Research

The primary difference between the original and the contemporary Scandinavian models of action research is that in addition to solving practical problems and contributing to general theory, the contemporary model also aims at making change and learning a self-generating and self-maintaining process in the systems in which the action researchers work. In addition to solving practical problems and contributing to general theory, the approach to action research typical in Scandinavia today aims at helping systems to develop a higher degree of self-determination and self-development capability so that organizational adaptation and learning continues after the researcher leaves the system. In other words, the key issue is how to promote self-sustaining organizational learning. The answer in the Scandinavian model is to develop new methods and roles for taking participants on as full partners in the research enterprise. This leads to fundamentally different relations between researchers and those supplying the data and relies on a different way of thinking about action research.

The project we have described is typical of a larger number of Scandinavian AR projects. The focus is on people who supply the data and participate in the research in such a way and to such an extent that they become full partners or co-researchers in running the research process itself. Participation in the sense of co-managing the research process and co-generating problem solutions and new knowledge is such a dominant element that this new form of action research can be called "participant-managed" action research. However, while dominant in Scandinavia, this form of AR is certainly not limited to this part of the world (Elden and Chisholm, 1993). Quite different developments in the United States have led to a similar model of AR under the name of "participatory action research" (Whyte, 1991). In short, contemporary action research focuses not only on helping people solve a particular practical problem but on increasing their problem-solving ability. If system self-improvement capacity is a goal, then system members must learn how to make sense of their own data in terms of their own language and in relation to their own perceptions and values. We have some indications that participants as co-researchers can provide much more valid data and useful interpretations (Elden, 1979b;

Whyte, 1989, 1991). An even stronger argument for participant control of knowledge generation is made by "participative researchers" (Hall, 1981; Brown and Tandon, 1983; Fals-Borda and Ralman, 1991).

In conclusion, a new and still emerging model of AR today in both Scandinavia and the United States has come from efforts to reinvent the basic elements and methods of action research from the 1940s (Elden and Chisholm, 1983; Chisholm and Elden, 1983). Power differences and the role of natural language and highly egalitarian forms of communication in the action research process are new issues in the design and conduct of action research. Furthermore, even though some terms are the same in the classical and contemporary models, they do not have the same meaning. Participation in AR, for example, now means full partnership in creating and using new knowledge. Epistemological egalitarianism in scientific method aims at participant learning and meta-learning, not just the solution to a scientific and practical problem. The important product here, in contrast to the classical model of action research, is participants learning how to learn to develop their own, more effective practical theories. Participants becoming better "practical theorists" is a key to democratization in the new Scandinavian model. Thus, the research enterprise itself needs to be as fully as possible co-determined and co-managed by external research experts and internal context-content experts working together in each phase of the AR process. The specific means may vary from case to case, with techniques ranging from "self-design," to "local theory," different forms of "democratic dialogue," "search conferences," multi-level networking, and other methods of what we have broadly referred to as "co-generative learning" (Elden and Levin, 1991). If AR is to contribute to democratization at work, the Scandinavian model suggests that action research should be organized and managed in ways consistent with democracy at work.

References

Aslaksen, K. *Organisational Development in the Processing Industry: Fiskaa Verk.* Oslo: The Norwegian Work Life Centre, 1991.

Brown, D., and Tandon, R. "Ideology and Political Economy in Inquiry: Action Research and Participatory Research." *Journal of Applied Behavioral Science,* 1983, *19* (3), 277–294.

Chisholm, R., and Elden, M. "Features of Emerging Action Research." *Human Relations,* 1993, *46* (2), 275–298.

Coch, L., and French, J. R. "Overcoming Resistance to Change." *Human Relations,* 1948, *1,* 512–532.

Crombie, L. "The Nature and Types of Search Conferences." *International Journal of Lifelong Education,* 1985, *4* (1), 3–33.

Davies, A., Naschold, F., and Pritchard, W. *Evaluation Report.* Oslo: Norwegian Work Life Centre, 1993.

Elden, M. "Conclusions from 28 New Action Research Projects in 8 European Countries." In International Council for Quality of Working Life (ed.), *The Quality of Working Life in Western and Eastern Europe.* Leiden, Netherlands: Nijhoff, 1979a.

Elden, M. "Three Generations of Work Democracy Experiments in Norway." In C. Cooper and E. Mumford (eds.), *The Quality of Working Life in Western and Eastern Europe.* London: Associated Business Press, 1979b.

Elden, M. "Political Efficacy at Work." *American Political Science Review*, 1981a, 5 (1), 43–58.

Elden, M. "Sharing the Research Work: New Role Demands for Participatory Researchers." In P. Reason and J. Rowan (eds.), *Human Inquiry: A Sourcebook of New Paradigm Research.* London: John Wiley, 1981b.

Elden, M. "Social Science for Policy-Making as a Learning Process." In J. F. Blichfeldt and T. Qvale (eds.), *Teori i Praksis: Festskrift til Einar Thorsrud.* Oslo: Tanum-Norli, 1983.

Elden, M. "Socio-technical Systems Ideas as Public Policy in Norway." *Journal of Applied Behavioral Science,* 1986, 22 (3), 239–255.

Elden, M., and Chisholm, R. "Emerging Varieties of Action Research: Introduction to the Special Issue." *Human Relations,* 1993, 46 (2), 121–142.

Elden, M., and Levin, M. "Co-Generative Learning: Bringing Participation into Action Research." In W. F. Whyte (ed.), *Participative Action Research.* Newbury Park, Calif.: Sage, 1991.

Emery, F., and Thorsrud, E. *Democracy at Work.* Leiden, Netherlands: Nijhoff, 1976.

Engelstad, P., and Gustavsen, B. "Swedish Network Development for Implementing National Work Reform Strategy." *Human Relations,* 1993, 46 (2), 219–248.

Fals-Borda, O., and Ralman, M. A. *Action and Knowledge.* New York: Apex Press, 1991.

Gjersvik, R. "The Construction of Information Systems in Organizations: An Action Research Project on Technology, Organizational Closure, Reflection and Change." Unpublished doctoral dissertation, Department of Organization and Work Life Science, Norwegian Institute of Technology, 1993.

Goode, L., and Bartunek, J. "Action Research in an Underbounded Setting." *Consultation,* 1990, 9 (3), 209–228.

Goranzon, B. *The Practical Intellect: Computers and Skill.* Paris: UNESCO Division of Philosophy and Human Sciences, 1991.

Gustavsen, B. *Dialogue and Development.* Assen/Maasticht, Netherlands: Van Gorcum, 1992.

Gustavsen, B., and Engelstad, P. "The Design of Conferences and the Evolving Role of Democratic Dialogue in Changing Working Life." *Human Relations,* 1986, 39 (2), 101–116.

Hall, B. "Participatory Research, Popular Knowledge, and Power." *Convergence,* 1981, 14 (3), 6–17.

Herbst, P. G. "Community Conference Design." *Human Futures,* Summer 1980.

Levin, M. "Creating Networks for Rural Economic Development in Norway." *Human Relations,* 1993, 46 (2), 193–218.

Lewin, K. "Action Research and Minority Problems." *Journal of Social Issues,* 1946, 2, 34–36.

Paalshaugen, O. *Means of Designing a Starting Conference.* AI-dok. 28/86. Oslo: Work Research Institute, 1986.

Pasmore, W., and Friedlander, F. "An Action Research Program for Increasing Employee Involvement in Problem-Solving." *Administrative Science Quarterly,* 1982, 27, 343–362.

Peters, M., and Robinson, N. "The Origins and Status of Action Research." *Journal of Applied Behavioral Science,* 1984, 20, 113–124.

Rapoport, R. N. "Three Dilemmas in Action Research." *Human Relations,* 1970, 23, 488–513.

Shani, A. B., and Pasmore, W. A. "Organization Inquiry: Towards a New Paradigm of the Action Research Process." In D. Warrick (ed.), *Contemporary Organization Development,* Glenview, Ill.: Scott Foresman, 1985.

Skule, S., and Levin, M. "Training Engineering Students in Management: Merging Theory and Practice." Paper presented at the 11th EGOS Colloquium, Paris, July 1993.

Sommer, R. "An Experimental Investigation of the Action Research Approach." *Journal of Applied Behavioral Science,* 1987, 23 (2), 185–199.

Susman, G., and Evered, R. "An Assessment of the Scientific Merit of Action Research." *Administrative Science Quarterly,* 1978, 23, 582–603.

Trist, E., Higgin, G. W., Murray, H., and Pollock, A. B. *Organizational Choice.* London: Tavistock, 1963.

Weisbord, M. (ed.), *Discovering Common Ground.* San Francisco: Berrett-Koehler, 1993.

Whyte, W. F. "Advancing Scientific Knowledge Through Action Research." *Sociological Forum*, 1989, 4 (3), 367–385.
Whyte, W. F. (ed.). *Participatory Action Research*. Newbury Park, Calif.: Sage, 1991.

MAX ELDEN is professor of administrative sciences, School of Business and Public Administration, University of Houston, Clear Lake; former postdoctoral fellow at the Work Research Institute, Oslo; director at the Institute for Social Research in Industry, Trondheim, Norway; and professor of organization and work life science, University of Trondheim.

REIDAR GJERSVIK is director of the Trondheim Center for Information Technology, Organization and Management at the Norwegian Institute of Technology.

This chapter describes action science, an action technology originally developed by Chris Argyris and later elaborated by Donald Schön, which focuses on changing beliefs that cause action.

Learning and Transforming Through Action Science

Karen E. Watkins, Tom J. Shindell

One approach to action research developed by Chris Argyris at Harvard with Donald Schön of MIT starts from a theory of human action. It posits that individuals act on the basis of their beliefs, and that the beliefs that drive action are largely unexamined and tacit. In this chapter, we discuss this cognitive approach to improving action by studying and changing human reasoning. We illustrate the use of this approach in higher education by describing the use of action science in a graduate program in adult education and human resource development. We then present examples of transformations made possible by the use of this action technology and analyze the outcomes at the individual, team, faculty, and program level.

The Theory of Action Science

Action science is a theoretical orientation that goes beyond a description of the process of critical reflection to offer a theory of intervention. It is intended to increase awareness of the puzzles and contradictions hidden in everyday interactions and to create the conditions for social change (Rogers, 1989). Action science begins with a view of human beings as designers of their actions in the service of achieving intended consequences. They make sense of their surroundings by constructing meanings, both cultural and individual, of their environment. These constructed meanings, in turn, guide actions (Argyris, 1982; Argyris, Putnam, and Smith, 1985). In action science, behavior is evaluated for consistency and validity against those internalized beliefs and meaning systems that individuals hold.

These meaning systems are the product of a rapid reasoning process, which itself may be flawed. Human reasoning is an artful, automatic process involving an escalation from the selective noting of observable events to abstracting about those events. Argyris uses a "ladder of inference" to make this reasoning explicit. The first rung of the ladder of inference is the directly observable behavior we select to which we pay attention; the second rung is the meanings we assign to this behavior; and the third is the action theory we derive from the lower rung interpretations.

Using the ladder of inference and sharing the process of creating meaning allows individuals to transform their behavior by understanding their often unexamined, rapid reasoning. For example, an instructor is asked if an assignment is mandatory or voluntary and replies, "I haven't lost my patience yet." What the instructor says is rung one on the ladder. Students might conclude that the instructor really means that the assignment is mandatory (rung two). They may construct personal theories regarding how to act thus: If the instructor answers a direct question with an ambiguous response, then she is getting angry and I had better do the assignment (rung three). This rapid movement through the ladder of inference from directly observable data to a personal action theory enables an individual to take quick and decisive action. Of course, the instructor may have meant something entirely different such as "I really haven't made up my mind. Things are going well as they are." This is where error often occurs. The work of action science is in making this reasoning visible so that it can be examined and ultimately changed.

Designing action requires that individuals develop a set of personal causal theories to describe and predict their world. These causal theories, termed "theories of action," include two types—espoused theories (those which individuals claim to follow) and theories-in-use (those which can be inferred from their actions). Thus, people actually hold two sets of theories: one about what they say they do and one about what they actually do. The espoused theory and theory-in-use may or may not be consistent, and an individual may or may not be aware of the inconsistency. While the espoused theory is conscious, the theory-in-use is most often tacit. A goal, then, of action scientists is to discover theories-in-use, particularly ones which inhibit or promote learning. The general model of action science is depicted as follows:

Values and Beliefs lead to → *Action Strategies,* which have → *Consequences*

Values and beliefs are those internalized values held by individuals and by cultures. *Action strategies* are the actions we take in order to enact values, and they have *consequences* for learning. When consequences are unintended, there may be a mismatch between action strategies and governing values. Action science describes two types of responses to mismatches. The first response is single-loop learning (also called Model I) in which action strategies are adjusted or changed (similar to trial and error learning). Single-loop learning is associated with a win/lose orientation, short-term gains, and a desire to control. The second response to a mismatch is double-loop learning (also called Model II), which involves the examination of values, not merely the adjustment of behavior. Incorporating critical reflection upon values and beliefs, double-loop learning is associated with having free and informed choice, valid information, and high internal commitment to new behavior.

Data Collection and Analysis in Action Science. Action science uses talk, a basic and important form of social action, as the raw data. Talk is the primary window into people's actions, values, and beliefs. This action technology begins with a sample dialogue—either an actual transcript, audio or video tape, or written reflection on what was actually said or done in a case. The case illustrates a problem the individual is having interacting with others or an anticipated dialogue that individuals believe may be difficult. Figure 4.1 depicts an action science case presented by "Larry" during the action science course described later in this chapter. Individual members of the group code the case to identify underlying themes and assumptions embedded in the dialogue. This coding makes the evaluations and judgments by the members of the group explicit. Larry's case is coded in Figure 4.1.

Group Data Analysis. Cases such as this one are discussed in groups. Group analysis of the data collected is the most powerful aspect of action science. Groups are made up of individuals, each of whom brings in a separate case. The group works to surface tacit beliefs held by the case writer that influence the outcome of the dialogue. This leads to exploration by the group of alternative strategies. For example: What does Larry believe that gets him into trouble? What else could Larry do in this case? Uncovering the tacit theories-in-use, discovering the gaps between espoused theories and theories-in-use, and examining the relationships among governing values, action strategies, and consequences is where most of the learning occurs for the individual case writer as well as for the group.

In the course of data analysis, thoughts and feelings of all participants are identified as they analyze the case. Attributions made by participants in the case as well as by group members are identified in the process of working through the case. The process is slowed down and individuals' here-and-now experience is shared. Inferential leaps that participants make when drawing conclusions from the data of the case are flagged, using the ladder of inference. Groups work from the directly observable data (dialogue) to agreed cultural meanings to identify the themes of the case. The process involves collaborative critical reflection and group members challenge the tacit assumptions of both the case writer and of other group members. The effect of this approach is that the case also becomes a vehicle for a "group case" in which all group members have an opportunity to get feedback on their ability to give feedback and on their reasoning while also experimenting with new behavior.

Data Mapping. Mapping is a vital instrument in action science, allowing learners to go beyond the details of a particular case to represent more generalizable patterns of behavior and belief systems. Maps are systematic depictions of governing values, action strategies, and consequences in a given case. In the course of the process of mapping, maps are considered incomplete until group participants offer confirming and/or disconfirming evidence. This evidence

Figure 4.1. Coding of Larry's Case

Note: The *italicized text* indicates codes and notations an action scientist might make about the underlined words and phrases considered significant in Larry's case.

Situation: I'm a 26-year-old intern at a manufacturing firm. I work in a small division, and organizationally I'm above a secretary and below a director. My boss, D, a director, has given me a great deal of underlined authority. In fact, I can prioritize and assign work to the secretaries as I see fit.

What leads L to define this "great deal" of authority? What is significant to L about being given this authority?

One secretary, S, is 47 years old and has been with the firm for years. I would frame her as a "plateaued" worker. One day, she took the afternoon off without telling me or my boss (who was out of town).

What did S say or do that led you to attribute that she is a "plateaued" worker?

My boss instructed me to speak to S and to use my judgment in "disciplining" her. My boss also told me to document everything. I was really worked up about what to say and how to say it. What follows is the conversation we had the next day.

This seems to be a dilemma. On the one hand, the boss tells L to "use his best judgment" while on the other, he tells L to "discipline" S. Does L see a dilemma?

Dialogue

What Was Thought or Felt But Not Said	What Was Actually Said
I hope this goes well. I hate underlined confrontations.	L: Good morning, S.
What leads L to frame this as a confrontation?	
I hope S does not get mad. I hope I handle it well. Ugh!	S: Good morning, L.
What would "handling it well" look like?	
I was furious! You left me in the lurch! I could have killed you. I felt like a fool. I didn't know where my secretary was; I had to type something! *Arbitration/evaluation* Oh sure! How could I see something you never wrote! You liar! *Arbitration/evaluation/judgment*	L: I want to talk to you. Yesterday, you left without telling me or D, and I really needed you. It really hurt my feelings. It made me feel like you don't care about me or respect me. S: I'm sorry, I thought you knew. I passed . around a note saying I would be gone. I guess you didn't see it. I'll have to make sure you see it next time. (pause) Anything else?
That's it? No groveling?	
What leads L to think that S should grovel?	

Wimp! I can't believe I didn't say how I felt!   L: No, I just wanted to tell you how I felt. Some <u>interventionist</u> I am!

What would a "real interventionist" have done?

Comments and Reflections: As it turned out, S had written a note that my boss, D, later found upon his return. Since the intervention, S and I have a very superficial relationship. Also, I was asked to recommend S for a raise. I did not. Now, I would like to explore these issues:

1. What prevented me from expressing my left-hand column?

What leads L to believe that he should express these thoughts?

2. Why do I feel like a rat?

What is rat-like in L's behavior?

3. What could I do better next time?

This is where learning in action science begins.

---

addresses the question of validity in the action science process. Both "here-and-now data" (descriptive maps derived from on-line interactions) and ideal depictions (normative maps derived from action science theory) may be included in maps. Maps are often "layered" or "nested." For example, at one level an individual trainer may map her behavior with regard to a persistent problem at work. At another level, there is a larger map of the organizational and cultural dynamics influencing her behavior. Figure 4.2 depicts Larry's map of his case.

Maps enable individuals to determine the ways in which their thinking about a situation leads them to act ineffectively. This map also depicts the way in which system problems interact with individual issues.

Teaching Action Science

At the University of Texas, action science is a theoretical framework for the graduate program in adult education and human resource development. A course was developed based on a similar one taught by Chris Argyris and Robert Putnam at Harvard University. The course is structured with an initial one- or two-day workshop to define key terms and to give students an initial "safe" laboratory experience. They look at cases of problematic interpersonal situations and analyze video and print cases. Initial practice includes learning to identify assumptions and attributions (their own and those reflected in the presented cases). They code a case (see Figure 4.1). Then they experience a fishbowl activity in which volunteers from the class join a group of trained action scientists in working a case by coming from the outer circle to an empty chair, making an intervention, and then moving back to the outer circle. These

Figure 4.2. Larry's Maps

	Model I Map (Less Learning)		Model II Map (More Learning)
Contextual Cue or Triggering Condition	When given responsibility that is inappropriate . . .	When confronting someone I don't want to make mad . . .	When given responsibility that is inappropriate . . .
Values and Beliefs	I should assume the responsibility anyway because I want to please my boss . . .	I should be indirect and say I'm "hurt," not "mad" . . .	I should trust my senses and say what I'm thinking and feeling . . .
Action Strategies	So I implement unreasonable requests like "disciplining" a secretary . . .	So I discuss my "safe" feelings and not my real feelings . . .	So I say that I think it is inappropriate and share my reasoning about it and inquire if my boss agrees . . .
Consequences in Behavioral World for Learning	Which guarantees that I will not please my boss.	Which guarantees that I don't really confront the other person and that I get mad because I did not share how I really felt.	Which guarantees an outcome that may please both of us.

brief attempts at working with a case are used as a laboratory to test various approaches to giving and receiving feedback. Role playing with a reluctant "learner/case writer" helps dramatize the difficulty in giving feedback without creating defensiveness.

From these workshop learning activities, we move into group sessions in which students work on each group member's case. Groups consist of four to six students and one or two action science facilitators (students who themselves have at least one semester of study of action science). Facilitators commit to an additional action science session with the course instructor to work each week on any problems they experience in their facilitation of the groups. The course is designed to incorporate practice in writing and analyzing cases. The cases allow students to experience difficult discussions about real events of high personal significance. Individuals are encouraged to accumulate cases around a common dilemma and to practice addressing the dilemma in real interpersonal situations. The interpersonal nature of this theory and its implementation in student groups necessitates first creating a climate of trust that includes critique. This climate enables students to come to the process prepared to question the validity and utility of the feedback given in these groups. Student facilitators function not as "experts" but as co-learners.

After the first workshop, the format of the remaining half-day sessions of the course is a combination of lecture and group work followed by community meetings of the entire class. In each of the remaining sessions, the entire class explores one concept of action science in depth prior to group meetings. Groups are encouraged to apply the concept in their analysis and to work with individual cases. Then, all of the groups come back together to discuss common issues or to prepare for the next class session.

In the small groups, case work follows Argyris' problem-solving model in which we *diagnose* a problem, *invent* action strategies to solve the problem, *produce* action to enact the strategies, and *evaluate* the results. Diagnosing the problem in the case means that individuals clarify the multiple meanings inherent in a given case (what the writer intended to convey and possible alternative interpretations). When the group exhausts this phase of the process, they develop a statement called a theory-in-use proposition, which encapsulates the dilemmas in the case. These propositions are if-then statements which specify the issue facing the individual, the actions the individual typically takes under these conditions, and the consequences of taking what are generally unproductive actions. We use a formula: "When _____ happens, I am afraid that _____ will happen, so I _____ which guarantees that _____ will happen."

The group subsequently works to *invent* an alternative approach that follows Argyris' theory of Model II action. In other words, they attempt to invent an approach the individual could take to promote learning and to reduce defensiveness in the case situation. This is equivalent to the action strategy phase. Argyris' theory stresses that there are many gaps between these inventions or intentions and actions.

Next, the group asks the individual who wrote the case to *produce* the alternative. This is the hardest part because the individual who brought the case is generally stuck in a particular mode of reacting, and it is extremely difficult to sincerely alter his or her style. Often, groups try again and again to suggest dialogue that they believe transforms the case. Sometimes each group member writes what he or she would say. The case writer then tries to say the words suggested by each group member until the case writer finds words with which he or she feels comfortable that also truly alter the control dynamic in the case.

Assignments consist of a composite portfolio or journal of the individual's reflections and a research paper. The reflections include the cases written, possibly a portion of the transcript of the group's discussion of the case, a description of the theory-in-use propositions given, and the various attempts at redesigning the case. The reflections summarize what the individual learned about his or her interpersonal skills and observations about the action science process.

The research paper asks individuals to select one of the key action science concepts such as defensive routines, the ladder of inference, Model I/II, and to read everything that Argyris wrote about it. This is reported and synthesized in the paper. Other options for the research paper include reading various critiques of action science, comparing action science to related group or action research strategies, or studying issues in action science such as that of competency acquisition vs. therapy.

Issues in Teaching Action Science

In our experience teaching action science, three critical issues continually reappear with each new group of learners: the seemingly therapeutic nature of action science; the problem of whether students experience free and informed choice; and the competence of those practicing action science. We discuss each issue individually.

The Therapeutic Nature of Action Science. Students often state that being in an action science group feels like "therapy." Argyris' view is that action science is not therapy, but skill learning (1968). However, when students are examining each others' reasoning and exploring the unexpressed feelings in situations they found interpersonally difficult, it is reasonable to expect that some therapeutic issues will be touched upon. We caution students that when the group feels like therapy, they need to make this known in the group and to set appropriate limits. We attempt to make this issue discussible so that novice learners will speak up when they feel threatened. Yet setting appropriate limits is difficult to do in the group. Argyris suggests that facilitators make minute-by-minute judgment calls in group settings when people are trying to learn new skills that are both experiential and interpersonal. It takes considerable skill both on the part of facilitators and the new learners to make appropriate calls when therapeutic issues come up, yet learning to do this is a necessary part of learning action science.

How Do We Ensure That Students Have Free and Informed Choice? Students often protest that participating in action science is both voluntary and mandatory. They remind faculty that one of Argyris' Model II values is "free and informed choice" and point out that some parts of the course are required, while others are voluntary or "free choice." In addition, although the course is not required, the placement of the course in a weekend program in which students took all courses in lock-step fashion makes it de facto a required course. We agree that this is a dilemma. It is also difficult to make collaborative decisions about course content, activities, and assignments when we do not share a common base of information. We concluded that enrollment and some types of participation are essentially free choice; yet students were correct that much of the course is mandatory.

Related to the concerns about whether students enjoyed the freedom inherent in Argyris' theory was the issue of how to prepare students to make an informed decision regarding whether to participate when they had no way to know what this experience would be like, in other words, to ensure *informed* consent. In an experiential learning situation, the learning is in the experience and it is very difficult to tell someone what to expect. They literally have to have the experience before they can decide whether or not to continue. We find this dilemma even more difficult to solve satisfactorily.

Facilitator Competence. A legitimate concern of individuals participating in an experiential learning activity is whether or not those who guide them know what they are doing. In an area as difficult as interpersonal skills learning, this is particularly important. While we had studied action science and practiced it for over six years, we were also aware that this did not mean that we would always act competently. The theory of action science suggests that people make errors when threatened and that they are often unaware of their errors. We strive to create a climate in which everyone's competence is evolving and no one is necessarily perfect. We hope that all of us are a part of a learning lab, and that students will help each other, their facilitators, and instructors become aware of any gaps in their practice. One way we create this climate is for both the instructor and the facilitators to write cases and to share them with the class and with their groups when things come up. For example, the instructor once shared the case presented in Figure 4.3.

When the instructor presented this case, both the students and the instructor were able to openly acknowledge the difficulty of teaching this material. Students appreciate having the work modeled and are more comfortable learning in an atmosphere in which the instructor is open to critique. This event also creates more of a culture of intimacy, which makes it easier to take risks.

Transformation in Action Science

Action science provides a means for change at the individual, team or group, instructor, and program or organization levels. It can be both powerful and unpopular because of its transformative nature. While transformations creating new perspectives may be desirable, this process is often difficult and painful.

At the individual level, action science case writers gain insight about what they do to create situations they do not want. As illustrated by Larry's case (Figure 4.1) and Larry's maps (Figure 4.2), Larry learned more about himself. Through this process, Larry has the potential to become more direct, more skilled in interpersonal situations, and more aware of errors in his reasoning about power and authority.

At the team or group level, action science can help teams and groups transform themselves. Action science can be used to transform the way in which a group learns together. Some facilitators share cases with their groups. Two facilitators, Ann and Sue, developed a map for one of their interventions in an action science group and shared the map with the group. Members of the group agreed that they observed the behaviors embedded in the map. Discussion of such maps develops a greater sense of trust and respect for the facilitators who are willing to be open about their unsuccessful facilitation. Further, the facilitators asked the group members to alert them when they were enacting the ineffective behaviors in the map. This creates a sense of release for members of the group who can now acknowledge openly that some of what the facilitators do seems "incompetent." Before sharing the map, the facilitators and group members were dealing with their power, control, and competence issues in ways that inhibited learning. After discussing and reflecting on their map, the facilitators and the group members were able to become more of a collaborative learning community. At the instructor level, action science transformed the relationship between teacher and students from one of provider of learning to one in which all were mutually responsible for their own and each others' learning.

Finally, at the organizational level, action science can facilitate transformation. In the program at the University of Texas, action science enables students and faculty to have many conversations that may not have been possible otherwise. Issues that were previously undiscussible now have both an ideology and a forum for expression. Specifically, on one occasion, students and program faculty met with Bob Putnam of Harvard University to discuss issues

Figure 4.3. Having Model I Feelings While Teaching Model II Skills

Model I: Dialogue	Model I: Instructor's Thoughts and Feelings	Model II: What Instructor Wishes She Had Said
Student: You've set us up to fail. Why don't you just show us how to do it rather than having each of us come up here and make fools of ourselves?	Ooh, that hurts. Does she really think that I would do that?	
Instructor: Because I know that unless you try the strategy that you think will work, you will continue to believe that it will, regardless of what we show you here. The key is to look at practice rather than strategy or intervention.	This is what I believe, but also what Argyris does when he teaches this.	*Instructor:* What is it that I said or did that led you to feel that I set you up to fail?
Student: I just knew that no matter what we did, you would not let us win. [Gives data to support this view.]	Win? Wow, this is so competitive!	[If student continues to say "just show us how to do it," explore further, using dialogue below]
Instructor: It feels so competitive, like it's really high risk to fail here.	Failure is high risk for me, too.	*Instructor:* I find myself in the following dilemma: How can we both look at and challenge skills we now take for granted as "working" while learning new skills that we don't yet know well enough for them to work?

in the program and developed a map of problems perceived by students. This map is illustrated in Figure 4.4.

Following the presentation and discussion of the program maps, the faculty and students began to change the program culture to one of greater directness and mutual accountability for problem solving. At the higher level of students' ability to effectively discuss difficult issues with authority figures, the learning capacity of all increased. Conversations about what faculty and the university were responsible for and what students might do to support the program led to greater role clarity and comfort with resource allocation. On the other hand, more resistant system problems were also identified and individuals were able to suspend blaming of each other for problems which none had created and

Figure 4.4. Program Map

	Model I *(Less Learning)*	*Model II* *(More Learning)*
Contextual Cue or Triggering Condition	When faced with the paradox of self-directedness versus formalized course requirements (syllabus) . . .	When faced with the paradox of self-directedness versus formalized course requirements (syllabus) . . .
Values and Beliefs	I should be a self-directed human being. . . . I should be goal-directed toward personal goals. . . . There should be no inconsistencies between espoused theories and theories-in-use in this program (well maybe some, but not major ones). . . . We should not have many conflicts in a well-designed educational program.	Real life is messy . . . and the outcomes are uncertain, but out of the ambiguity come opportunities for learning and growth.
Action Strategies	I complain, do the course requirements, try change of requirements and give up after trying once.	I learn to differentiate between my responsibility and that of others through a mutual dialogue with members of the learning community using advocacy and inquiry.
Consequences in Behavioral World for Learning	I don't get the changes I want; I feel frustrated, so then I collude with other students by talking to them and not the professor and I ensure that I will not be self-directed.	I receive clarification regarding my role and responsibility to myself and to the learning community.

none of the group could single-handedly solve. Action science is one of the few action technologies that has the broad transformative potential outlined here.

Implications of Action Science for Adult Educators

While facilitators have developed many strategies to aid reflection in action science, there is no substitute for strong group process skills. While difficult issues may surface in any of the action technologies described in this book, this one so directly zeroes in on problematic interpersonal situations that it can be highly volatile. It is not unusual for individuals to experience strong emotions and for facilitators to be challenged to think on their feet. Some feel as though they are in therapy groups with this intense focus on their behavior. In short, this is not for everyone. Caution is appropriate.

On the other hand, the tools of action science are not at all mysterious. Anyone can write a case. Analyzing critical incidents of behavior to determine whether or not one is combining advocacy, inquiry, and illustration when under threat is easily accomplished without the need of a group or a specially trained facilitator. Maps of action strategies with suggested alternatives can be developed by collecting cases in writing or through interviews. As a guide to aid individual reflection or as a tool to conduct needs assessments or organizational diagnoses, these tools are highly useful.

Moreover, the theoretical framework which undergirds action science is normative. This framework suggests ideal conditions for dialogue. Action science would be limited if it argued only for a culture change without speaking to the systemic and social norms that produced the current culture. Yet, because it does hope to transform these norms and because it has evolved specific tools and strategies that may produce these changes, it has greater potential than many other action technologies to actually bring about these changes.

Action scientists tend to work within the boundaries of organizational systems. As a result, they generally first change individuals' behavior and that of groups before working to produce lasting fundamental transformations of the organizational culture. Action science has the ability to deal with often difficult yet reoccurring themes or issues such as power, empowerment, and control at the individual, team, leader, and organizational levels as illustrated in the cases presented in this chapter. The promise of producing changes and dealing effectively with difficult issues that are reflected and mirrored by different levels within organizations is the profound appeal of action science.

References

Argyris, C. "Conditions for Competence Acquisition and Therapy." *Journal of Applied Behavioral Science,* 1968, 4 (2), 145–177.

Argyris, C. *Intervention Theory and Method: A Behavioral Science View.* Reading, Mass.: Addison-Wesley, 1970.

Argyris, C. *Reasoning, Learning, and Action: Individual and Organizational.* San Francisco: Jossey-Bass, 1982.

Argyris, C., Putnam, R., and Smith, D. M. *Action Science: Concepts, Methods, and Skills for Research and Intervention.* San Francisco: Jossey-Bass, 1985.

Rogers, R. P. *Reflective Learning About the Workplace: An Action Science Study with Adult Children of Alcoholics.* Ann Arbor, Mich.: Dissertation Abstracts International, 1989. (University Microfilms No. 22219369)

Shindell, T. J. *Toward a Theoretical Analysis of Action Science.* Ann Arbor, Mich.: Dissertation Abstracts International, 1994.

KAREN E. WATKINS is associate professor of adult education, University of Georgia, and former director of the graduate program in human resource development, University of Texas at Austin.

TOM J. SHINDELL is assistant executive director of the Academy of Human Resource Development.

If persons who generate knowledge through participative inquiry shared it in the public arena, our formal knowledge base would be enriched. This chapter is intended to help participatory researchers disseminate their findings.

Collaborative Inquiry for the Public Arena

Group for Collaborative Inquiry; thINQ

Many forms of participative research methodologies have emerged during the last few decades that reflect values of holism and egalitarianism (Reason, 1994). Because people usually engage in participative inquiry for their own empowerment or problem-solving, they rarely share their "findings" outside the group. Thus, the rich body of knowledge generated in such inquiries remains largely unavailable to others. In occupational fields like adult education, where the experience of practitioners and constituencies should be part of the knowledge-base that informs theory, this lack of access to what is learned in participative inquiries impoverishes the field and marginalizes the insight of constituencies and practitioners (Group for Collaborative Inquiry, 1993).

The authors have been engaged in participatory research, but unlike typical participatory researchers, our goals include making a contribution to formal knowledge by sharing our findings through public discourse. We call this process "Collaborative Inquiry for the Public Arena." We hope that by describing what we have learned, we will encourage other participatory researchers to contribute to formal knowledge and to theory-building. Before proceeding, we introduce ourselves:

The Group for Collaborative Inquiry is a group of four women adult education scholar-practitioners, joined together to study learning, change, and social action. Geographically spread from New York to California, the group meets periodically in a member's home, sharing travel and food costs equally. When the group formed in 1990, members intended to write a book by working

---

Because our work reflects a shared construction of knowledge, publications and presentations are listed under our group names.

57

collaboratively, but did not articulate a group vision of collaboration. Group understanding of how to work collaboratively with the intention of constructing knowledge and theory for public discourse has evolved slowly from experience.

thINQ is a group of three women and two men who are adult education doctoral students finishing a dissertation project about collaborative inquiry. At the time of this writing, the group has been working together for two and one-half years. Initial ideas about collaborative inquiry came from Peter Reason's model of cooperative inquiry (Reason, 1988) and from the dissertation adviser's experience as a member of the Group for Collaborative Inquiry. thINQ's experience with the process has generated knowledge far beyond initial understanding.

We have organized this chapter into sections. First we describe concepts that define the essence of our common experience, then we share stories from each group's history that illustrate how these essential concepts have been lived within our groups. We conclude by speculating about how our experience might be useful to others.

Defining "Collaborative Inquiry for the Public Arena"

Collaborative inquiry for the public arena is defined as: the systematic examination through dialogue of a body of data and lived experience by researchers whose intentions include the construction of formal knowledge that can contribute to theory. Iterative cycles of dialogue within the group and actions taken by individuals outside the group create the opportunity for new data and life experience to enter the flow of group meaning-making continuously.

In living this dialogic process, our groups have identified three axioms as follows:

AXIOM 1: *The co-researchers' lived experience is equal in importance to formally collected data.*

The importance of including the researchers' lived experience is axiomatic to participatory research in general and is not limited to our particular experience of collaborative inquiry for the public arena. However, the task of formal knowledge-making requires special attention to validity. We believe that the methods of meaning-making most congruent with the values of participatory research are the methods of hermeneutics, phenomenology, and feminism (thINQ, 1994; Group for Collaborative Inquiry, 1993). Within this literature the participatory researcher can find guidance for mixing lived experience with more formally collected data (Moustakas, 1994; Spiegelberg, 1970).

AXIOM 2: *Knowledge created in the group belongs to the group.*

Knowledge is created in a constant stream of interaction among group members over an extended time period. Each time the group convenes, each individual brings new experiences and insights accrued since the group's last meeting. Each time the group adjourns, individuals go into the world with new insights and experiences. Because researchers embrace a holistic view of knowledge that includes their lived experience, the collaborative inquiry group represents a dynamic, ever-changing intersection of individuals' perspectives in which boundaries between personal and group knowledge become blurred.

The idea that knowledge created in the group belongs to the group may seem self-evident to practitioners of participative methodologies, but the context of communicating in the public arena is the factor that makes living this axiom difficult. In societies that value competition and reward individuals for achievement, blurred boundaries between individual and group knowledge-making are not easily accommodated. We believe that groups who want to practice collaborative inquiry for the public arena will struggle with tensions between individual voice and group ownership. The group's ultimate capacity depends on successful resolution of these tensions. Our groups have symbolized our intentions regarding this second axiom by adopting group names to represent us in the public discourse.

AXIOM 3: *Each co-researcher must be equal in contribution and commitment.*

A group's capacity to embrace the second axiom depends on its lived experience of the third. This third axiom refers not only to shared responsibility for group task and maintenance roles, but more complexly, it refers as well to a quality we call "whole-person" engagement. By this we mean that the group's dialogue as well as its general purpose must engage each individual similarly. Affective connection to dialogue and commitment to purpose are as important as mutual intellectual interests.

Two Examples of Collaborative Inquiry for the Public Arena

We now move to sharing our experience. thINQ's story is narrated in the collective voice of "we," while the Group for Collaborative Inquiry's story is told from member Gwendolyn Kaltoft's perspective. Although the authors of this chapter did not plan this contrast in voice, we immediately recognized its value when we shared initial drafts. The ever-present dance between "we" and "I" is at the heart of collaborative inquiry for the public arena.

thINQ's Experience with Six Collaborative Inquiries. The five members of thINQ are students in the Adult Education Guided Independent Study program at Columbia University's Teachers College. In June of 1991, a faculty member invited our class to consider participating in a collaborative inquiry project as dissertation research. After a brief description of what might be involved, she suggested summer reading (Reason, 1988; Guba, 1990) and an exploratory meeting at the start of the fall semester.

Five of us eventually responded to the invitation. We met monthly during the Fall semester, engaged in what Reason (1988) describes as the initiation and contracting phases of collaborative inquiry. In these phases it is important "to be sure that the project the initiator wants to do is one that makes sense to potential group members" (p. 21) and "to explore carefully the different expectations people bring" (p. 23). Throughout our fall meetings we were ascertaining our acceptance by the group, assessing whether our voice would be heard or silenced by others. Also, as John Bray later remarked, "we were trying to determine whether we could trust the others to deliver the goods." This issue was especially important because we were embarking on dissertation research. Individual progress would be inextricably linked to the work of others. We agreed that we would attend all meetings and be prompt with assignments.

Early in our work, when Joyce Gerdau was selected to represent her state at a national conference, she asked the group for our opinion about missing part of our regularly scheduled meeting for that month. In the subsequent discussion, this decision was turned back to Joyce to be made based on her personal priorities. By not giving permission, the group was pressing Joyce to act out her priorities. She said immediately, "I'll cancel the presentation." This was a watershed event in our history. Not only had pressure been placed on Joyce, but all of us felt we had to honor this commitment in the future.

In December 1991, all officially committed to the inquiry and we began audio-taping and transcribing our meetings. From that date, with two exceptions, we have met monthly. Our meetings are often two-day weekends, but have included meetings as long as six days.

The Federated Design. To guide our work we created a definition: "Collaborative inquiry is a process of repeated episodes of reflection and action through which a group strives to answer a compelling question of importance to each participant." We decided that we could best study collaborative inquiry by participating in it ourselves, but that we could not create dissertation-level research from the experience of simply studying ourselves as one five-person group of collaborative inquirers. We decided that each of us should initiate our own collaborative inquiry group. Thus, each of us participated in two collaborative inquiries—our own group of student researchers, which we began to call the core inquiry group, and groups each of us convened, which we refer to as the field groups.

"thINQ" as a Symbol of Collaboratively Produced Knowledge. To underscore the collaborative nature of our enterprise, we adopted "thINQ" as a group name for our publications. Our group is diverse in learning styles, gender, and areas of professional practice. Out of this diversity comes both tension and richness of perspective. Each of us feels free to borrow from and build upon the work of other group members. Our experience of the inquiry is collectively owned. We assume that insights are often nurtured within the group before they are named. We arrive at insights through reflection on what happens in the group and on the events which our collaboration has set in motion.

The importance of group ownership of ideas emerged early in our experience. In one draft of his dissertation proposal, Lyle Yorks cited an earlier draft of Joyce Gerdau's proposal, thus giving her credit in the traditional academic style. Our dissertation adviser challenged Lyle York's underlying assumption, and our group discussed the issue explicitly (thINQ transcript, Mar. 1992 meeting, pp. 294–295):

LYLE: I have no problem with everything being considered collective. I thought I heard us agree that we take things and sort of absorb them. . . .

ANNETTE: . . . You don't always know where the ideas come from. That was something I thought we said from the beginning—the important issue for me in being part of this.

JOHN: The transcript wars (laughter).

This ethic of collective ownership of meaning is important for two reasons. First, it is important that we not withhold ideas, reserving them for personal use. Second, competition for leadership within the group impairs collaborative effort.

ANNETTE: It almost gets kind of competitive. . . .

LINDA: The issue of competition. We live in a society that is incredibly competitive. As much as we want to collaborate and work together, it's something we have to struggle with. . . .

JOYCE: . . . I also see this as an insight about the collaborative inquiry process. . . . that if you're working cooperatively, competition can override cooperation and vice versa. It's nice to know that we are anticipating . . .this . . .issue in working together.

JOHN: . . . If it's in a group . . . the group owns the idea actually. [thINQ transcript, Mar. 1992 meeting, p. 296]

The openness created by group ownership is important to the learning process (thINQ transcript, Jan. 1993 meeting, pp. 2361–2363):

ANNETTE: More and more I see how I learn better in groups . . . hearing phrases from other people triggers certain things that make me think about something in another way. It sets me off in another direction. . . .

JOYCE: We feel like we're becoming trusting enough of one another. . . as a result of using this structure, because we feel freer. We feel more open . . . more dynamic as people. . . .

Establishing these norms of collective ownership of ideas and shared influence was not easy. We learned (and are still learning) how to participate with each other. Respect and openness cannot be mandated; they need to be established through experience. The process of learning how to participate with each other started during the initiation and contracting phase and is continual.

Our inquiry has involved cycles of convergence and divergence as we come together to engage in dialogue and make meaning as a group, then return to our respective homes to write, reflect, and take further action. These cycles make for varying tensions between the individual and the group. We achieve individually held meaning, which is tested within the group. When our ideas find acceptance and become part of the group's meaning-making process, there is a feeling of affirmation. Conversely, there can be a sense of disappointment or frustration when individual meaning does not resonate with others in the group. These are times when adopting an attitude of critical subjectivity and demonstrating a willingness to examine one's assumptions becomes crucial. The process is aided by a sense of trust and support.

Sometimes, an individual whose meaning is not resonating with the group will decide to "let go." How one decides to let go of a particular perspective is a complicated process. We have learned to "let go" because we came to realize that letting go is not "giving up." We have learned to understand the temporality of the process. If the issue under discussion is critical to our future direction, and we cannot reach agreement on the point, we postpone the issue, tabling it for future discussion. Sometimes, this is done subtly through changing the topic or taking a break. Other times, it is done with formal agreement. We have learned that if an idea is important, it will come around again after our discussions have created a perspective that makes its importance clear to all of us. An important factor in helping us learn to let go is the lack of ego posturing in our group. One has to be willing to have one's ego work on behalf of the group, not one's self.

Maintaining a Posture of Critical Subjectivity. As we strive to answer our inquiry question, we are working with text created from our own experience— in other words, transcripts of the meetings of the six inquiry groups and our own learning journals and observations. We seek to create formal knowledge from these texts by engaging in a constructivist approach. In doing so, it is essential to avoid self-delusion and produce trustworthy interpretations.

Our field groups, through "member checks," were asked to assess the extent to which our writings are consistent with their experience. We have adopted some of the safeguards commonly employed against groupthink: devil's advocacy, considering alternative explanations, and submitting our work to the judgment of others familiar with what has transpired, but who are not directly involved. This latter role was played by our dissertation sponsor. Other checks include returning repeatedly to the experience itself via the text. In reexamining our interpretations, we see whether they are colored by preexisting personal agendas.

Impact of Collaborative Inquiry on the Individual. When we met with Peter Reason, he expressed his personal view that one marker of valid collaborative inquiry is the extent to which the process disrupts the personal lives of the researchers. This comment is both a statement on validity and a description of how collaborative inquiry can impact the inquirer. Each of us has changed significantly as a result of this experience, as have members of our field groups. Space has not permitted us to tell these stories of personal change and empowerment, but in the Group for Collaborative Inquiry's story which follows ours, Gwendolyn Kaltoft speaks about the interrelatedness of personal growth and group experience. We feel she speaks for us as well. Here is Gwendolyn's story of writing for the group:

The story I narrate is both about the Group for Collaborative Inquiry and about me. While thINQ's story recounts the evolution of group skills and identity, I speak of personal evolution and the interconnectedness between my growth and the group's. This story is about the relationship between the individual struggle and the group struggle with finding both individual voice and group voice.

The process of writing this story began in February 1994 in San Francisco at a meeting of the Group for Collaborative Inquiry. To prepare for writing this chapter and other work, the four of us spent a weekend in our tradition of being with one another, telling stories, and examining our cumulative experience. During that weekend we distilled from our experience the axioms presented in this chapter. We also divided responsibilities. Since I volunteered to write the section of this chapter that was to be a story about our group, I then went home and wrote this story from my perspective.

Writing has been, and continues to be, a fundamental key to our learning. Writing has linked our understanding of the relationship between each individual's knowledge and the knowledge of the group.

One of the dramatic memories I have, which gives me a clear comparison of my current and earlier relationship to my own writing voice, is a writing experience from 1991 in which I wrote on behalf of the Group for Collaborative Inquiry. In the next few pages I tell that earlier story and contrast it with how I currently feel about myself and the group as we write together.

In our first year of working together, we submitted an abstract and were accepted for the Adult Education Research Conference. I offered to write the paper that was to be submitted. At that time, there were six of us, and we were meeting in Brooklyn Heights, New York. I remember sitting on the floor in the back sitting room of the big brownstone house surrounded by the other members of the group and feeling an internal flood of conflict and confusion. I was afraid that I couldn't really do it, and yet I was proud that the others would invest me with the responsibility. I had an inkling of a sense of duty, accompanied by an agonizing sense that I had something to prove. And deeper inside, I sensed I was casting an anchor to a belonging in the group. With all these feelings lingering in my unspoken awareness, I asserted my commitment to write the paper. Within the five-minute period that it took for me to make the offer and for the group to accept it, my body remained calm, my face did not distort, and my conscious mind was unaware that my confidence was shaky.

When I returned home to the Midwest, I settled into organizing my approach to writing. I thought that consulting each member would be consistent with our group's emerging beliefs about collaboration. So, because we were six people separated by thousands of miles, I began to call each member to talk about her ideas.

Some time into the third phone call, I became aware of my anxiety. With each new conversation, I heard the individual voices of my collaborators representing divergent views. As I called back group members in order to refine the themes we were trying to present, I heard what seemed like disagreements. These individual voices sounded like people speaking different languages—trying to communicate, with no common ground for understanding. I fell limp with my job as interpreter. My body, mind, and spirit felt invaded with what I perceived as representatives from the academies of sociology, feminist thought, organizational development, social change theory, personality development, and adult education. I felt conflicted, clogged, and full of fear. I obsessively taped the phone conversations and listened to those tapes over and over again. I tried repeatedly to write, but the words looked like an unfamiliar foreign language on the screen of my computer. I walked back and forth between my computer and my kitchen—looking for something to eat but never finding anything that satisfied me. I took long walks searching the Iowa countryside for answers, but could not see them, and I called the group members again and again. The divergent voices persisted. Nothing helped me to subdue the anxiety, which felt like ice running through my veins that surged with the pounding of my heart.

I tried desperately to analyze my fear and anxiety, but my thoughts translated those feelings into believing that I simply was not up to this task. I argued with myself: "I can write! I completed my dissertation and have received many complimentary remarks from people I admire." My self argued back: "This is different. This paper will represent the ideas of all six people in our group, and I am responsible for the reputations of all those people." So, I tried again, but constantly found myself stuck in my attempts to create links between what I perceived as my collaborators' conflicting views. Rationality failed me. I was in a perpetual state of anxiety until the paper was done. When it was complete, I sensed that it was "half baked" and this feeling fueled my sense of my own mediocrity. I don't remember any awareness of a concept of "my own voice" or a desire to put a part of me into the paper. I felt the paper had very little to do with me, but rather with my understanding of the ideas of others. I felt alone.

The reconstruction of that experience has been hard and painful work.

In contrast to writing the 1991 paper, my current experience of writing this story has been dramatically different. The difference is hard to describe because it requires capturing a long and freeing process in very few words. In contrast to the overwhelming constriction I felt while writing the 1991 paper, this writing has been a truly liberating experience. It has been a journey through which I have moved and learned, not alone, but *with* the whole group. Our four years of working together have given me confidence with knowing my contribution to the group, and our process of learning together has nurtured us as a dynamic whole group. This time I have not worked alone to translate and meld the ideas of individuals. Annie Brooks, Elizabeth Kasl, and Kathy Loughlin each spent a great deal of time helping me work out my feelings and synthesize my ideas into our ideas. This time the group has worked together to find *our* words in *my* individual and personal voice.

The difference between the two experiences is at least partially explained by three insights I discovered along the journey of writing this story. When I/we set out to write the 1991 paper, we as a group were very young. Since we were in our first year of meetings, and the AERC paper was our first, we had no history of writing together nor any tradition for working out divergent perspectives. As I reconstructed the 1991 story, I relived the anxiety I had experienced. After weeks of writing and rewriting, I finally asked myself, what was this anxiety in 1991 signaling? I knew my feelings of fear and inadequacy had been partially rooted in my personal history and in my lack of experience in these public academic realms, but I believed there was something more.

As I sat at my computer with my head in my hands in deep reflection, I had a crystallizing awareness. I suddenly understood that the anxiety was not only a signal of my own feelings of being threatened, but it was a signal that the group also had felt threatened. I had been the barometer for our group's state of being. Awareness of our connections flooded my thoughts—myself and the group, our individual perspectives and feelings, our concerns that each of our ideas be represented. My understanding began to integrate our multiple realities, issues of group ownership, equal responsibility, and mutual commitment—none of which had been articulated in our group space of being together. All those issues danced around the knowing of our group as a dynamic organism.

Shortly after I recorded this insight, I decided to reread the 1991 paper to further my understanding. Lo and behold, there on the last page was a section entitled "Emergent Issues." I was astounded! We had articulated the issues. We had written " . . . we must resolve [these issues] in order to continue our collaborative commitment" (Group for Collaborative Inquiry, 1991, p. 118). The issues included: ownership or authorship, speaking on behalf of the group or representing the group in the public arena, unrecognized personal assumptions that impede communication, choices about whose language is to be used, different thinking and learning styles, lack of unity in understanding the group task, accommodating personal agendas, influence of personal life events, commitment to the group and to our vision, and constraints of time, money, and resources.

I find it very difficult to share the magnitude of my feelings with having discovered that list of "emergent issues" at the end of this current writing journey. I had read the 1991 paper in preparation for writing this story, but I had simply glanced at the list, disregarding it for what I thought to be more substantive content in the body of the paper. When I read the list this time, having just recorded my crystallizing awareness about our connectedness, our concerns, and my role as the group barometer, I had a third insight.

My final insight knits together the whole of the 1991 writing experience and this current story-writing. I realize that the act of writing, individually and together, not only brings our voices into the public arena, but also helps us come to understand what we know.

In 1991 we didn't have the capacity for the deeper writing and understanding that we now experience because we had not yet collectively lived out our list of emergent issues. It all made sense. My anxiety and the group's anxiety cautioned difficulties ahead. We had inklings that resolving the emergent issues would be a complex and painful process, and our anxiety signaled a sensible fear of the unknown. Now that we have walked the journey of group life together, we have lived the struggles we anticipated when we identified the emergent issues, named what we know, and are able in both our personal and group voices to tell others about what we have learned.

Conclusion

Through stories from our experience, we have tried to communicate the complexity of meaning intimated in the three axioms. In the first axiom, we note that issues of validity are of special importance in collaborative inquiry for the public arena. In its story, thINQ describes procedures that support the group's critically subjective consciousness. We also note in our presentation of axiom 1 that we believe the methods of phenomenology, hermeneutics, and feminism offer the most appropriate guidance for formal knowledge-making associated with collaborative inquiry. In these methods, recursive writing is a basic activity for testing validity. Within the complexity of groups writing together, this recursive writing embraces both individual efforts and group statements. thINQ reports how cycles of convergence and divergence test validity and generate new meaning. Gwendolyn Kaltoft refers to cycles of writing and rewriting when she describes how other group members helped her to tell group ideas in her personal voice. These cycles are part of what we call the ever-present dance between the "I" and the "we." We want to emphasize that the tension of this dance can be destructive, but it also holds the potential for enormous creativity. It is our experience that the act of writing collaboratively both tests validity and supports more generative meaning-making.

The idea developed in axiom 2—that knowledge created in the group belongs to the group—challenges groups who are embedded in cultural values of competition and individual achievement. thINQ explains that the key to learning to "let go" is a willingness to have personal ego work on behalf of the group, and that learning to let go has been made easier as the group learned that "letting go" is not the same as "giving up." Gwendolyn Kaltoft's story encapsulates a four-year journey by the Group for Collaborative Inquiry as it struggled to find the relationship between individual and group voice. Neither of our groups has found it easy to live out the challenge of this second axiom, but we have found Time to be our friend. Time has helped us find mutual trust, appreciation of each person's unique gifts, and the exhilaration of group learning and accomplishment that gives us the will to persevere.

In axiom 3 we write about equality of commitment and engagement. Early in thINQ's history, the way in which Joyce Gerdau met the challenge to act out her priorities set a precedent that is among the most critical factors supporting the group's success. Gwendolyn Kaltoft describes knowing that she was anchoring herself to the group when she offered to write the 1991 paper in spite of shaky confidence. Although our stories have more explicitly illustrated equality of commitment than equality of engagement, our experience is permeated with the power of what we call whole-person engagement.

In summary, the process of taking group knowledge into public discourse is generative for the group's continued learning. It challenges individuals whose day-to-day lives embed them in structures that value individual achievement and competition. Its promise as a process that can empower individual members is more fully realized through long-term engagement.

References

Group for Collaborative Inquiry. "Democratizing Knowledge: A Model for Collaborative Inquiry." In *32nd Annual Adult Education Research Conference Proceedings*. Norman: University of Oklahoma Center for Continuing Education, 1991.

Group for Collaborative Inquiry. "Democratizing Knowledge." *Adult Education Quarterly*, 1993, *44* (1), 43–51.

Guba, E. (ed.). *The Paradigm Dialog*. Newbury Park, Calif.: Sage, 1990.

Moustakas, C. *Phenomenological Research Methods*. Newbury Park, Calif.: Sage, 1994.

Reason, P. (ed.). *Human Inquiry in Action: Developments in New Paradigm Research*. Newbury Park, Calif.: Sage, 1988.

Reason, P. "Three Approaches to Participatory Inquiry." In N. Denzin and Y. Lincoln (eds.), *Handbook of Qualitative Research*. Newbury Park, Calif.: Sage, 1994.

Spiegelberg, H. "On Some Human Uses of Phenomenology." In F. J. Smith (ed.), *Phenomenology in Perspective*. The Hague, Netherlands: Nijhoff, 1970.

thINQ. "Phenomenology as an Interpretive Frame: The Evolution of a Research Method for Understanding How Learning Is Experienced in Collaborative Inquiry Groups." In *35th Annual Adult Education Research Conference Proceedings*. Knoxville: University of Tennessee, 1994.

GROUP FOR COLLABORATIVE INQUIRY is a group of practitioner-scholars who write and learn together, working to create a collaborative model for scholarship within the academy. Group members are Annie Brooks, Gwendolyn Kaltoft, Elizabeth Kasl, Kathy Loughlin. We honor the contributions of two past members: Molly Daniels and Trudie Preciphs.

THINQ group members John Bray, Joyce Gerdau, Linda Smith, Lyle Yorks, and Annette Weinberg Zelman came together to do dissertation research with adviser Elizabeth Kasl.

Participatory action research is claimed to be a process in which knowledge collectively generated is used for the development of strategies for social change.

Participatory Action Research: Principles, Politics, and Possibilities

Nod Miller

My aim in this chapter is to examine the principles and practices of participatory action research and to assess the significance and usefulness of this research paradigm for adult educators. I shall illustrate my outline of the elements in participatory action research with reference to examples of work that I have conducted.

Defining Participatory Action Research

The term "action research" is used to refer to a bewildering array of activities and methods. Many British writers use the terms "action research" and "participatory action research" synonymously, seeing participation as an essential element of action research projects. For example, Cohen and Manion (1989) see action research, which they define as "small-scale intervention in the functioning of the real world and a close examination of the effects of such intervention," as "usually (though not inevitably) collaborative [and] . . . participatory" (p. 217). Another writer, at the end of a lengthy discussion of research methods for teachers, states that he has "used the terms 'applied research,' 'action research' and even 'evaluation' as virtually interchangeable. I explained earlier that I was doing this in order to hold to a rather loose and generalized conception of what I took to be an identifiable approach to educational research, not wishing to be drawn too closely into fine distinctions between different approaches within that overall research direction" (Walker, 1989, p. 195). Walker includes the activities of teachers who work in isolation and regularly reflect on their own practice (perhaps with the help of a consultant or "critical friend") under the heading of "self-evaluation: action research mode." He sees teacher-researchers who engage in systematic reflection in the context of "a coherent group who meet regularly" as conducting "'classic' action research" (p. 199). Another writer defines action research in terms of its contrast with conventional positivist social science:

> Conventional laboratory-derived research styles seek to minimize the degree of involvement between the researcher and the researched in the interests of objectivity. This falls foul of much that is known about the change process and of conditions facilitating change. The discrepancy is not surprising as the task of conventional pure scientific research is to describe, understand and explain— not to promote change. Coming to terms with the dual 'understanding' and 'promoting change' roles calls for a different view of research. This perspective owes much to the work of Kurt Lewin, who coined the term ACTION RESEARCH for it. [Robson, 1993, p. 438]

My own perspective of participatory action research differs; the following section presents the origins of my approach.

Defining My Own Practice

I am a white woman and I am forty-four years old. I am a feminist and my social origins are in the working class. I work in a university department of education and manage a center for research and teaching in the education of adults. I am a sociologist and I teach postgraduate courses in media and communication studies and adult education, working with students from many different nationalities, cultures, and occupational groups. In the work in which I have been engaged over the last fifteen years in the field of adult education, I have generally defined myself as being engaged in action research with strong elements of participation. I have used the terms "participatory research" and "action research" as embracing the same activities (Miller, 1986). I see action research as having two defining characteristics: first, researchers participate in the research as both subjects and objects of the research; second, there is an explicit intention to bring about change through the research process. Research activities and the understandings derived from them are negotiated with all those involved in the research process. In the model which I have used, conventional distinctions between researchers and researched are blurred and the importance of researchers making their political stance explicit is emphasized.

My own practice and the theoretical models that inform and shape it have a variety of influences. One important source of influence has been Lewin's work on action research. Inextricably linked to this are the theory of learning encapsulated in the experiential learning cycle and the model of democratic learning lived out in the T-group. In the Lewinian experiential learning model (Kolb, 1984) it is assumed that, for example, group behavior is best understood from the experience of participating in groups and observing group processes as they occur. Theory-building about group behavior takes place on the basis of reflection on that experience. Abstract conceptualization and generalization are followed by experimentation with new forms of behavior, which in turn become the object of further reflection and theory-building. T-groups, in which participants learn about group processes and social structures as a result of experiencing and reflecting on their own here-and-now behavior in a group, were 'discovered' by accident during a conference on intergroup relations organized by Lewin and his associates for community leaders, teachers, and social workers in Connecticut in 1946. Lewin saw the use of small groups aimed at accomplishing personal change as being linked with a widespread process of social change. Social scientists were seen by Lewin as important agents of social change, and his interest in understanding and attempting to resolve intergroup conflict arose out of his own experience in Nazi Germany, where he had experienced anti-Semitism at first hand. One of his colleagues described how Lewin saw "cooperative action research as a way for human beings to solve their problems and manage their dilemmas" and as a means of uniting research, education, and action "in the elimination of social injustice and minority self-hatred and in the wise resolution of intergroup conflicts" (Benne, 1976, p. 316).

The way I conceive my work as a social researcher has been strongly influenced by C. Wright Mills's notion of the sociological imagination, which he defined in the following way: "a quality of mind that will help . . . [people] to use information and to develop reason in order to achieve lucid summations of what is going on in the world and of what may be happening within themselves. The sociological imagination enables its possessor to understand the larger historical scene in terms of its meaning for the inner life and the external career of a variety of individuals . . . the sociological imagination enables us to grasp history and biography and the relations between the two within society" (Mills, 1970, p. 11–12). I believe that it is this potential for linking the personal and the structural, individual life histories and collective social movements, private and public worlds, which makes sociology such an exciting and powerful discipline. And yet Mills's clearly expressed insight seems often to get lost in the way in which sociology is written and taught. Certainly much of my early experience as a student of sociology led me to doubt whether the subject had much at all to do with my life experience. In my practice as an adult educator, I have tried to develop approaches to the facilitation of learning that are consistent with the goal of "linking history and biography."

Another influence on my practice and identity as a researcher has come out of contemporary feminist theory, particularly that strand in feminist thought that places emphasis on the importance and presence of the personal within research experience and practice (Stanley, 1990; Stanley and Wise, 1993). Such work stresses the importance of acknowledging the way in which autobiographical experience shapes research questions and approaches, and of locating the researcher at the center of what is to be researched. Feminist research entails the clear intention of changing the social world, particularly in terms of existing asymmetrical gender relations. As Shulamit Reinharz suggests in her examination of feminist action research, "The purpose of feminist research must be to create new relationships, better laws and improved institutions" (Reinharz, 1992, p. 176). My own experience as a woman, a feminist, and a member of a working-class family, and my work with colleagues and students from a wide range of nationalities and ethnic groups have led me to a commitment to the promotion of social justice and social change.

Current Debates About Participatory Action Research

An important contribution to current debates about the politics of participatory action research has been made by McTaggart (1991), who provides a very full account of the principles that he believes are essential to this form of research practice. He sees the goal of "the improvement of the understanding, practice and social situation of participants" (p. 169) to be of paramount importance, stating that "If we decide that something is an example of participatory action research, we are suggesting that it is likely to have improved the lives of those who have participated" (p. 169). He acknowledges Lewin as the inventor of action research and describes the Lewinian model as involving a spiral of steps, each of which requires the planning, acting, observing, and evaluating of the action. He argues that Lewin's deliberate overlapping of action and reflection was designed to allow changes in plans for action as people learned from their own experience, and summarizes action research as "the way groups of people can organize the conditions under which they can learn from their own experiences and make this experience accessible to others" (p. 170).

McTaggart distinguishes between "participation" and "involvement," suggesting that authentic participation in research means "sharing in the way research is conceptualized, practiced, and brought to bear on the life-world. It means ownership—responsible agency in the production of knowledge and the improvement of practice" (p. 171). Participatory research is seen as different from the "kinds of research which typically involve researchers from the academy doing research on people—making people the objects of research" (p. 171). Participatory action research, according to McTaggart, engages "academics" and "workers" in collaborative research projects where both groups take responsibility for the development of theory and practice. He goes on to outline nine principles of participatory action research. These included the interrelationship of individual and collective concerns of research participants; an emphasis on changing the culture of working groups involved in the research—that of other groups to which participants belong and that of the broader society of which such groups are part; the importance of spirals of learning in which action and reflection are central; the unifying of intellectual and practical concerns; the importance of the involvement of "workers" in processes of knowledge production; the interrelationship between research processes and political action; and the development of theory out of the research process. Although McTaggart's analysis is useful in identifying some important features of participatory action research and in raising some crucial ethical and political issues concerning its practice, his paper leaves a number of questions unanswered.

To begin with, it is not clear from his account how the process of participatory action research works in practice. It would certainly not be easy to design a participatory action research project on the basis of the description he gives. Although he outlines two examples of his "principles in practice" in two research projects carried out in northern Australia, these are not sketched in sufficient detail to bring the projects to life. The degree of his own involvement in these projects is not made explicit. Furthermore, it is not clear how participatory action research is distinguished from other research paradigms, which are also characterized by a rejection of positivist models and methods and which are concerned with the promotion of change. These include new paradigm research (Reason and Rowan, 1981; Reason, 1988); transformative research (Beder, 1991); experiential analysis (Reinharz, 1983), and other varieties of feminist research (Reinharz, 1992); autobiographical or biographical research (Stanley, 1992), and participatory research (Hall, 1981; Tandon, 1981). It is often difficult to see what is particularly distinctive about each of these models since a good deal of common ground is covered in descriptions of the various approaches. Sometimes it seems that the establishment of new paradigms has more to do with staking out academic territories than with furthering theory or practice. I have made this observation in more detail in the case of transformative research (Miller and Armstrong, 1991). McTaggart, while acknowledging the important contribution of Kurt Lewin, nevertheless feels that "the Lewinian conceptualization has some limitations. Lewin did not spell out the nature of action research in much detail. But it seems from his writings that his interest in the theory of group dynamics overshadowed what we would now see as fundamental to participatory action research, the commitment that all participants actually do research for themselves" (1991, p. 170). This remark seems to be based on an assumption that Lewin's concern with group dynamics is a diversion from the central activity of action research. In fact, as Lewin's associates make clear, the T-group is precisely the site in which action research as defined by Lewin takes place. Proponents of the T-group method see the learning which takes place in the T-group laboratory in terms of action research and regard the collective, collaborative element in the method as central: "Action research [in the T-group laboratory] is an application of scientific methodology in the clarification and solution of practical problems. It is also a process of planned personal and social change. In either view, it is a process of learning in which attention is given to the quality of collaboration in planning action and in the evaluation of results" (Benne, Bradford, and Lippitt, 1964, p. 33).

In characterizing the groups typically involved in participatory action research as "academics" and "workers," McTaggart imports further problems. There seems to be an uneasy suggestion embedded in his analysis of academics "helping" the workers despite the fact that great emphasis is placed on the sharing of power in the research relationship and on the importance of egalitarian principles. A final difficulty arises out of McTaggart's stress on "life improvement" as the desired and intended outcome of participatory action research. It is important to recognize that improvement cannot be taken to be the same thing as change; furthermore, it cannot be assumed that there will be consensus within or between groups about what constitutes life improvement. Moreover, it is difficult to predict outcomes of participatory action research projects with any degree of accuracy. Participants bring their own concerns and agenda items to any such project, and it is rarely, if ever, possible to control what results from it. In any case, if the work is to be truly collaborative and participatory, it is undesirable for any one individual or subgroup to attempt to exercise such control.

A Participatory Action Research Project: The Mini-Economy

McTaggart's analysis helps to highlight some of the important questions that arise in relation to the theory and practice of participatory action research. At this point I propose to examine these questions further by referring to an example from my own research, which I hope will illustrate some of the problems and possibilities in participatory action research.

I have been engaged in a wide variety of action research projects over the course of the last fifteen years, including events sponsored by professional adult education and group relations organizations in Britain, simulation exercises with groups of broadcasters and policy makers, workshops for international bodies in adult education in the U.S.A., Canada, Thailand, and Australia, conflict resolution projects in Western Australia, and a participatory research workshop for adult literacy workers and community activists in Brazil. Examples of work of this kind are described more fully in my writings (1991, 1993). This work has built on the theory and methodology of the T-group laboratory and has been designed to explore aspects of inequality and difference through participatory action research methods. My intention has been to set up frameworks within which participants can explore social structural relations as they are patterned by, for example, gender, age, and social class at an interpersonal and small group level. In some cases I have defined my activity in terms of political intervention in groups and organizations to which I belong. Some aspects of the approach that I have developed are exemplified in an event called the Mini-Economy, which took place in Leeds, England, in 1985. The aim of the event was to explore the relationship between economic structures and social behavior; its intention was to address such questions as how economic structures influence types of personal relationships, responses to others, and feelings about self; how people treat others who are richer or poorer than they are; how economic structures can be influenced; and whether or not it is possible to achieve consensus in a stratified society. The design of the event, which I organized with Jim Brown, a colleague particularly interested in economic development in small communities, drew on elements of the T-group laboratory, with its emphasis on learning through observation of group behavior as it happens and on the creation of opportunities to experiment with new behaviors and structures. The event had a number of features in common with the Scandinavian "Mini-Societies" organized by Gunnar Hjelholt in the early 1970s, which were also experimental events derived from the group relations laboratory designed to explore intergroup interaction and to further understanding of contemporary social issues. The event was advertised widely among those groups that we considered would have a particular interest in the issues to be explored. These included teachers and researchers in the social sciences; community activists, particularly those working in the voluntary sector or with workers' cooperatives and in local economic development; human resource development specialists and trades unionists; and unemployed people.

The event attracted thirty-four participants, including management consultants, teachers, social workers, academics, community and cooperative development workers, several unemployed people, and a nun. There were sixteen men, seventeen women, and one female child; two of the participants were black, of African origin, while the rest were white. Participants lived together four days in a residential conference center. We attempted to draw in a wide range of participants in terms of income by creating a fee structure whereby each participant paid to attend the residential weekend according to her or his "real life" income. The fees ranged from £10 ($15) for those on a very low income, to £75 ($112.50) for high-income earners. We created a currency called the *bongo* for the event, and on arrival each participant was issued a checkbook and allocated a daily allowance of bongo units, which matched what she or he had paid as a fee. Thus participants who had paid £75 were given 75 bongos a day, those who had paid £55 received 55 bongos a day, and so on. The daily allowance could be used to purchase such basic resources as meals, bedroom accommodation, tea and coffee, alcoholic drinks, and use of the lavatories. The idea was for the community to be faced with the problem of how to deal with the fact that some individuals did not have the resources to afford a bedroom, while others had enough resources to exist very comfortably. Participants were obliged to make decisions about and implement changes in the economic structure.

My co-organizer and I acted as civil servants within the community, running the bank, taking room bookings, and selling tickets for meals. Prices were arranged so that someone receiving 45 bongos a day would have enough to buy a bed in a dormitory, three meals, four cups of coffee, and a couple of drinks in the bar. At the outset of the event we advertised various jobs to give participants the opportunity to supplement their basic income by becoming, for example, bank tellers, tea and coffee sellers, or lavatory attendants. As it turned out, roughly half the participants had an income above 45 bongos a day and could therefore live above subsistence level, while the other half received less than 45 bongos and therefore faced some form of economic hardship. Approximately one-third of the participants received 75 bongos a day, their relatively affluent position contrasting starkly with that of the three "paupers" existing on a daily income of 10 bongos.

The event ran from 5:00 P.M. on Friday to 4:00 P.M. on Monday. The only predetermined features of the event, apart from the economic structures described above, were two large group review periods each day, to allow for reflection on the process and experience of the event, fixed mealtimes and bank opening hours. Something of the flavor of the weekend was captured neatly in a description given by one participant shortly after the event: "During the first 24 hours we managed to condense five centuries of social change; we lived through capitalism, revolution, socialism, and feudalism."

In the early hours of the first morning of the Mini-Economy, a group of participants (a combination of high-income men and low-income women) calling itself the Kitchen Occupation Group broke into the kitchen and announced its intention of remaining there until redistribution of wealth took place in the community. Breakfast was made available to all participants free of charge. Shortly after this, a meeting of what became known as the People's Assembly took place and a revolutionary spirit spread through the community. Subcommittees were set up to plan a new economy. Soon after this, the bank records were stolen and the civil servants were forced to resign. The People's Assembly announced the establishment of a new currency called the *bingo*. Everyone was allocated an equal income, and meals and bedroom space were distributed free of charge. For a short time, an atmosphere of euphoria prevailed and participants addressed each other as "comrade." Gradually it dawned on people that there was little on which to spend the bingo units.

At this point (twenty-four hours into the event), the kitchen staff of the conference center let it be known that they were no longer prepared to serve meals until participants did some "real" work. Calling themselves "the lords of the kitchen" and operating with the slogan "the feeders are leaders," they recruited two participants to organize a work schedule and announced that anyone who refused to work would be refused meals. They reinstated the civil service as king and queen (making it clear that this was to be a monarchy with only symbolic power), and other participants were appointed queen mother, bishop, and high priestess. Rumors of plans for a maypole celebration began to circulate. On the third day of the event, the community divided along gender lines, and impassioned discussion of the inequities of "men's work" and "women's work" ensued. The kitchen staff resigned from their positions as lords of the kitchen. The importance of a "social economy" was discussed since at that time social relationships constituted the most valued commodity in the community. Later there was experimentation with a "risk economy," where participants' social contribution was defined in terms of their willingness to experiment with risk-taking.

Participants spent most of the final day of the event in small groups, attempting to make sense of their experience of the event. The event ended with a large group review meeting attended by all participants, which was characterized by confusion and long silences.

Some Issues Raised by the Mini-Economy

The first issue raised by this event is that of the unpredictability of outcomes from work of this kind. Our intention in the Mini-Economy was to further understanding of economic and social inequality and, by enhancing understanding, to promote change at both individual and societal levels. However, it turned out that we were unable to predict even the changes that took place inside our microcosmic society. In view of this, it would have been surprising if we had been able to forecast accurately the changes that individuals might experience in terms of their understanding, attitudes, and behavior as a result of their participation, let alone the larger-scale changes that might be wrought in the groups to which participants belonged in their lives outside the event— which might in turn contribute to more widespread social change.

Despite the fact that participants in the Mini-Economy generally shared a concern with working to bring about social change and to combat social and economic inequalities, there was no consensus among them during or after the event about priorities for change or the appropriate strategies by which changes could be brought about. Recognizing the unpredictability of outcomes from work of this kind, and the difficulty of establishing agreement about the direction and nature of desired social change, talk of "improvement" as a necessary result of participatory action research is simplistic.

A second issue concerns the degree of control exercised by participants over the setting of the agenda for the research. In the case of the Mini-Economy, my co-organizer and I were responsible for designing a structure and setting up aims for the event. Our expectation and intention was that others would set their own agenda. An unresolved question is that of the extent to which the research remained "ours" because of our role in planning and designing the structure. Some people perceived us (inside the event) as acting in an oppressive fashion. At times it was unclear (both to ourselves and to others) whether we were administrators, facilitators, or researchers. We found it difficult to draw clear boundaries around our roles. An important piece of learning was the need for greater clarity in this area.

I stated earlier that one defining characteristic of my model of action research was the participation of the researcher as both subject and object of the research. This is easy to say, but doing it can be painful and difficult. Although as a feminist researcher I recognize the importance of acknowledging the place of emotion in the research process, I have found that reflecting on and coming to terms with one's own behavior, motivations, and attitudes is not easy. This was illustrated powerfully in the aftermath of the Mini-Economy; my co-organizer and I cried for several hours immediately after the event. During the course of the Mini-Economy it became apparent that, while some participants clearly defined themselves as engaged in participatory research, there were others for whom the term "research" carried connotations of rats in mazes and of immoral experimentation with human subjects. Those of us who are based in the academy are expected as part of our work to engage in something called research, but many people outside academic life would not describe their own learning from experience, the development of their understanding or the actions they take to effect change as "research." Perhaps the demystification of what counts as research should be one of the goals of participatory action research. The question of whether it is a necessary criterion for all involved in a project to agree that it should be labeled "participatory action research" for it to be participatory action research remains unresolved.

One other difficulty that emerged in the course of the Mini-Economy was that of engaging in systematic reflection in the midst of intense and involving experience. This is something with which I continue to struggle in the course of my own research and experiential learning and in my efforts to facilitate the learning of others. I have found the work of David Boud and his associates helpful in suggesting models of reflection (Boud, Keogh, and Walker, 1985), but the practical problems in ensuring adequate time and designing appropriate structures for reflection persist.

Questions are sometimes raised about the nature of the reality experienced within events like the Mini-Economy. I have been asked this question a number of times: "Isn't what you're describing just a kind of role-play or simulation?" There was some debate about where "reality" began and ended during the course of the Mini-Economy. One participant suggested early on that, during the review sessions, the action in the event should be, in effect, frozen. This suggestion was not so much rejected; rather it seemed that as we were enacting what felt like "real" behavior; we simply could not stop and start our action to order. Gurth Higgin, a social scientist involved in the organization of one of the Mini-Societies referred to earlier, concludes his account of it in the following way: "If it was all only role-playing, it certainly didn't feel like it. But then it doesn't in everyday life, does it?" (Higgin, 1972, p. 663). This observation might just as easily have been made of the experience of participants in the Mini-Economy.

Implications for the Practice of Participatory Action Research

What emerges most clearly from the above account may be the tensions and contradictions in the participatory action research paradigm. In the course of writing this chapter, my doubts about the possibility and usefulness of defining principles of participatory action research with precision have been amplified rather than allayed. This is not to argue for a return to positivist social science or to suggest that I would wish to abandon the struggle to devise and implement appropriate and innovative research strategies in the field of adult education. Further description and analyses of participatory action researchers' experiences that acknowledge the emotional as well as the intellectual content of the research process and its challenging nature as well as continuing dialogue between researchers may help to illuminate some unresolved questions about research practice.

Elsewhere, I have described a piece of participatory action research in which I was involved where another participant declared that his experience of this event was "the least useful day I have ever spent" (Miller, 1991, p. 178). Although this was not quite the end of the story as far as this workshop or that participant went, the anger and confusion evident in this statement caused me to reflect a good deal on the ethics, politics, and unpredictability of this form of inquiry. Clearly, participatory action research is not experienced as uplifting and rewarding by all participants. Researchers adopting this approach need to recognize that outcomes may be unexpected and sometimes painful for some or all participants.

My own experience is that participatory action research is fulfilling, frustrating, messy, confusing, and exciting—just like "real life," in fact. It is also difficult to contain within clear time boundaries. Since the research is explicitly concerned with the promotion of change, the process continues beyond the time and space in which participants are explicitly engaged in the work. Although definition is difficult and the process is hard to capture and delineate, participatory action research offers potential for its practitioners to reach understandings about the complexity of experience and to develop strategies for change. There are circumstances where nothing else will do.

References

Beder, H. "Mapping the Terrain." *Convergence,* 1991, *24* (3), 3–8.

Benne, K. D. "The Process of Re-education: An Assessment of Kurt Lewin's Views." In W. G. Bennis, K. D. Benne, R. Chin, and K. Corey (eds.), *The Planning of Change.* (3rd ed.) Troy, Mo.: Holt, Rinehart & Winston, 1976.

Benne, K. D., Bradford, L. P., and Lippitt, R. "The Laboratory Method." In L. P. Bradford, J. R. Gibb, and K. D. Benne (eds.), *T-Group Theory and Laboratory Method.* New York: Wiley, 1964.

Boud, D., Keogh, R., and Walker, D. (eds.). *Reflection: Turning Experience into Learning.* London: Kogan Page, 1985.

Cohen, L., and Manion, L. *Research Methods in Education.* (3rd ed.) London: Routledge, 1989.

Hall, B. L. "The Democratization of Research in Adult and Non-formal Education." In P. Reason and J. Rowan (eds.), *Human Inquiry: A Sourcebook of New Paradigm Research.* Chichester, England: Wiley, 1981.

Higgin, G. "The Scandinavians Rehearse the Liberation." *Journal of Applied Behavioral Science,* 1972, *8* (6), 643–663.

Kolb, D. A. *Experiential Learning: Experience as the Source of Learning and Development.* Englewood Cliffs, N.J.: Prentice Hall, 1984.

McTaggart, R. "Principles for Participatory Action Research." *Adult Education Quarterly,* 1991, *41* (3), 168–187.

Miller, N. "A Workshop on Action/Participatory Research." In M. Zukas (ed.), *Papers from the Sixteenth Annual Conference of the Standing Conference on University Teaching and Research in the Education of Adults (SCUTREA).* Leeds, England: SCUTREA, 1986.

Miller, N. "Changing Conference Culture: Exploring Social Processes Through Structured Experience." *Studies in Continuing Education,* 1991, *13* (2), 167–179.

Miller, N. *Personal Experience, Adult Learning and Social Research: Developing a Sociological Imagination in and Beyond the T-group.* Adelaide: Centre for Research in Adult Education for Human Development, University of South Australia, 1993.

Miller, N., and Armstrong, P. "A Dialogue on the Curious History and Dubious Future of Transformative Research." *Convergence,* 1991, *24* (3), 42–49.

Mills, C. W. *The Sociological Imagination.* Harmondsworth, England: Penguin, 1970. (Originally published 1959.)

Reason, P. (ed.). *Human Inquiry in Action: Developments in New Paradigm Research.* London: Sage Publications, 1988.

Reason, P., and Rowan, J. (eds.). *Human Inquiry: A Sourcebook of New Paradigm Research.* Chichester, England: Wiley, 1981.

Reinharz, S. "Experiential Analysis: A Contribution to Feminist Research." In G. Bowles and R. Duelli Klein (eds.), *Theories of Women's Studies.* London: Routledge & Kegan Paul, 1983.

Reinharz, S. *Feminist Methods in Social Research.* New York: Oxford University Press, 1992.

Robson, C. *Real World Research: A Resource for Social Scientists and Practitioner-Researchers.* Oxford, England: Blackwell, 1993.

Stanley, L. (ed.). *Feminist Praxis.* London: Routledge, 1990.

Stanley, L. *The Auto/Biographical I: The Theory and Practice of Feminist Autobiography.* Manchester, England: Manchester University Press, 1992.

Stanley, L., and Wise, S. *Breaking Out Again: Feminist Ontology and Epistemology.* London: Routledge, 1993.

Tandon, R. "Dialogue as Inquiry and Intervention." In P. Reason and J. Rowan (eds.), *Human Inquiry: A Sourcebook of New Paradigm Research.* Chichester, England: Wiley, 1981.

Walker, R. *Doing Research: A Handbook for Teachers.* London: Routledge, 1989.

NOD MILLER *is head of the Centre for Adult and Higher Education at the School of Education, University of Manchester, England.*

*A basic framework for popular education is elaborated as an emerging
action technology and pedagogical alternative. This framework is
based on the key ideas of Paulo Freire's works and illustrated by two
experiences at the grassroots level.*

Popular Education: Building from Experience

Carlos Alberto Torres, Gustavo Fischman

> When you live among us, don't mock us by trying to be exactly like
> us. We know you have more money than we do. We know you can
> always leave. We know you are used to different foods and ways of
> doing things. Live a balance. Live in the middle between what you
> have come from and where we are. By doing that we know you
> don't stand away, removed from us and yet we can recognize that
> our way is not the only way. Walk with us and learn before you are
> too critical. We must walk together in friendship.
> —Stelck (1994, p. 183)

The Origins of Popular Education

Popular education as an alternative pedagogical movement and as an action
technology arose from a political and social analysis of the living conditions
of the poor and their outstanding problems (such as unemployment, mal-
nourishment, poor health) and attempted to engage the poor in individual and
collective awareness of those conditions. Popular education bases its practices
on collective and individual previous experiences (understood as previous
knowledge) and stresses collective work rather than individualistic approaches. The notion of education in popular education refers to the concrete
skills or abilities such as literacy or numeracy that popular education projects
are intended to instill in the poor. The projects strive to arouse pride, a sense
of dignity, personal confidence, and self-reliance among the participants.
While popular education was originally developed as a nonformal strategy
sometimes opposed to the education sponsored by the state, some current

NEW DIRECTIONS FOR ADULT AND CONTINUING EDUCATION, no. 63, Fall 1994 © Jossey-Bass Inc., Publishers projects are being originated by governments. For example, Colombia and the Dominican Republic have sponsored projects related to integrated rural development; and Nicaragua, through the collective of popular education, has initiated projects directed toward adults as well as children.

Popular education originated in Latin America and soon extended to other regions throughout the world. Popular education shows an enormous potential and dynamism, allowing different perspectives within the paradigm. This multiplicity of perspectives empowers practitioners and enriches their praxis and the performance of the popular education movement in general. Despite the diversity in popular education, there is no doubt that Paulo Freire has had a significant influence on its practice. In the next section, we discuss the foundational work of Paulo Freire, particularly his influence on critical pedagogies in North America. The following section describes and analyzes the implementation of popular education in two different political and historical contexts: a literacy program with migrant population in Los Angeles today and a project with a first nation people in Argentina during the 1980s. Finally, in the last section, we discuss the theoretical and practical lessons that can be learned from popular education as an action technology.

Paulo Freire and the Foundations of Popular Education

The work of Paulo Freire has become a trademark of popular education projects in Latin America and elsewhere. Freire has put together a synthetic yet dialectical approach to structures and social agency in education. He has done so at the level of meta-theory by discussing our basic commitments regarding the nature of social reality, human individuals, and history and society. At the level of educational theory, he has explored how these epistemological and political commitments inform the dynamic relationships between knowledge, power, and education.

For Freire and popular education advocates, knowledge is a social construct; it is a process and not merely a product. This is important because Freire's pedagogy emerged as a critique of the traditional (authoritarian) educational paradigm, but also of its challenger in the region, positivist pedagogy, which was gaining ground in Latin America during the 1950s and 1960s. Popular education inspired by Freirean pedagogy proposes a nonauthoritarian but directivist pedagogy for liberation. The teacher is at the same time a student, and the student is at the same time a teacher—even though the nature of their knowledge may differ. As long as education is the act of knowing and not merely transmitting facts, students and teachers share a similar status and are linked through a pedagogical dialogue characterized by horizontal relationships.

The educational agenda is not necessarily carried out in a classroom, but in a "culture circle." Emphasis is placed on sharing and reflecting critically upon learners' experience and knowledge, both as a source of material for analyzing the "existential themes" of critical pedagogy, and as an attempt to demystify existing forms of false consciousness. Insofar as the state and the school system represent instances of mediation and control, pedagogues of liberation are suspicious of schools, and perhaps most state institutions. Only recently has the notion of public popular schooling been advanced by Freirean pedagogues in the context of Brazilian debates on school autonomy (Torres, 1994).

A central tenet of popular education is the notion of "conscientization" or critical consciousness. With his insightful yet complex language, Freire argues: "Inasmuch as we are conscientizing, so much are we unveiling reality, so much are we penetrating the phenomenological essence of the object that we are trying to analyze. Thus, critical consciousness means historical consciousness" (Freire, 1980, p. 74). Thus, literacy training, nonformal education, and public popular schooling developed by liberation pedagogues have an explicit conscientization goal, and particularly the development of class consciousness as historical consciousness.

The implications of Freire's proposal and popular education for schooling are vast. For example, the idea of utilizing the needs of the communities as a prime material for the design of vocabulary for the literacy programs simultaneously undermines the power of "curriculum experts," school administrators, and state bureaucracy, while giving back to the individual teacher control over what goes on in the classroom. Cultural politics implies that curriculum control and teacher autonomy are part and parcel of a crucial cultural conflict in society—a conflict around the definition of which knowledge, what culture, and what subjectivity is more relevant for the fabric of society. This conflict has serious implications for school organization and administration, and hence the outcome of the struggle for school autonomy will define both the nature of public schooling and of the democratic pact in liberal societies.

Obviously, in the context of debates over school excellence for international competitiveness vis a vis equality of educational opportunity, or proposals stressing adapting schools to the needs of industry and the marketplace, the research and policy agenda of liberation pedagogy and popular education will be disruptive of any school "ethos" based on the premises of corporate culture and the technical discourse of managerialism (Apple, 1993).

Freire's *Pedagogy of the Oppressed* influenced the origins of participatory action research in Latin America and along with critical and feminist approaches has constituted a central reference for popular education. Popular educators, social scientists, teachers, and community activists have questioned conventional social and educational research approaches based on positivist and empiricist assumptions. Based on dialectic, phenomenological, and hermeneutical perspectives, popular education is supported by a political understanding of educational praxis. Therefore, the overall political intentions of popular education should come as no surprise. In the words of Freire, "Popular education postulates the effort of mobilizing and organizing the popular classes with the goal of creating a popular power" (Torres, 1986, p. 59). It aims toward improving educational praxis and social change. Thus, teachers, scholars, and community activists are interested in the potential for implementation of popular education as an action technology, and eventual difficulties in the design, implementation, and operation of popular education projects. We turn now to discuss two experiences of popular education.

Two Stories of Popular Education

Popular education is flexible and adopts a great variety of forms. It starts from the premise that education is a political act, and that education plays a central role in social change and conscientization. A central feature of popular education is the practice of collective self-criticism, a form of continuing evaluation. This relates to the search for an alternative education model that is technically effective, ethically sound, and politically feasible. This moral, technical, and political standpoint is an imperative for popular educators who, as pedagogical and social actors, challenge the unequal and oppressive pedagogical—and nonpedagogical—relationships so prevalent in many educational settings.

A project with immigrants in Los Angeles that we chose to call El Refugio—a fictitious name—and a project with first people nations in Argentina provide examples of popular education as action technology. The analysis of these two cases offers illustrations of popular education in diverse geographical, social, and ideological scenarios, and discusses different stages in the process of conceiving, planning, and implementing this educational model.

El Refugio is a literacy program that serves a predominantly working-class Central American community in Los Angeles. The project with the Mapuche, a first people nation in the Province of Buenos Aires, Argentina, is a clear example of how popular education can benefit a small number of people by attending to crucial aspects of their ethnic and cultural identity. In addition, the Argentinean project is an example of how popular education can be implemented in ways other than its traditional involvement with literacy training programs.

El Refugio de Los Angeles: Popular Education and Critical Literacy for Latino Immigrants. By 1985, an estimated 60 million adults in the United States—or one out of three—was illiterate. More specifically, approximately 20 million adults could not read or write at all, and nearly 40 million people had literacy skills at or below the 5th grade level. A decade later, while the number of absolute illiterates has fallen, the number of functional illiterates has dramatically increased, as a government study shows. In fact, the total number of illiterates (including functional illiterates who are reading at or near elementary school levels) are estimated to be over 80 million people, half the adult population of the country (Kozol, 1985).

As in the rest of the world, illiteracy is unevenly distributed in the United States, both geographically and socioeconomically. Inner cities, poor regions, and minority groups such as non-native English speakers, Latino/as, African Americans, and women represent a disproportionate number of the illiterate population. Not surprisingly then, illiteracy in East Los Angeles, an area with mostly Latino/a population, is a particularly pervasive phenomenon. This is the social context in which El Refugio, one of the many community-based organizations, sought to develop a critical literacy model drawing from the tradition of popular education and the framework of critical pedagogy (Giroux and McLaren, 1989; Pruyn and Fischman, 1994).

El Refugio offers a comprehensive literacy program, both in English and Spanish. Initially, the program organized three English as a second language and two Spanish levels. Each class met four times a week for two and a half hours with a literacy focus. Then they met a fifth time in order to pursue other social and political activities. Courses are free. Students and teachers are encouraged to participate in an elected board that plans and evaluates the program. There have been attempts to increase the number of students in the program. When the program started, it had only two levels of ESL and two of Spanish with about seven students in each. In the second year, a third level of ESL was opened and the enrollment grew to an average of twelve to fifteen students per level. An underlying assumption of the program is that Latino immigrants not only bring their work force and their culture into the country (and into the program), but also their experience with different action technologies.

The program's mission or philosophical statement lists three major project objectives:

1. To assist in the promotion of a coherent organization in which decision-making mechanisms are participatory
2. To forge linkages across and within social classes to gain greater economic and economical power for the poor
3. To assist in designing strategies that shift concentrations of power to the poor.

The program's critical assumptions are as follows:

1. The oppressed have their own set of values and ideas born out of daily struggle for survival.
2. This project is envisioned as an opposition force to the formal institutions of education that have stifled criticism, imposed silence and passivity, and made the masses of our community "objects" rather than "subjects."
3. The project supports the idea of an intrinsic relationship between education and politics. In that sense, the project makes no pretense at neutrality and holds that education can either reproduce the existing power relations and unequal society or serve to emancipate students from the economic and political forces that subjugate them.
4. To achieve these goals, the project does not adhere to a fixed curriculum. In that sense, teachers must act as facilitators.

These statements clearly reflect the program's goals and direction, yet they also indicate some contradictions. First, in assumption 1, the phrases such as "the oppressed have their own set of values" suggest an exaltation of the culture of the community as pure and uncontaminated by the larger society. Yet assumption 2 states that the community has become dehumanized or alienated. It is difficult to guide a project with such extreme and contradictory assumptions.

Second, education is seen as a quasi-omnipotent tool. The learning process has become a kind of zero-sum game in which there is a transparent and simple division between losers and winners. Thus, the only problem for teachers and community activists is simply to choose the right side—in other words the Latino community because of its "purity and noncontradictory ideals." This appears the logical starting ground for the politics of liberation. However, an underlying assumption is that there are no intra-community conflicts based on gender, ethnicity, national or regional origin, or age.

Third, the notion of popular education suggested in objective 2 seeks the pursuit of class alliances, while objective 3 shifts the purpose dramatically and proposes the empowerment of the poor as a central tenet. However, it is unlikely that those in the upper socioeconomic strata or holding hegemonic positions will voluntarily accept a drastic redistribution of power favoring the poor, nor will they facilitate a radical participatory process with similar goals. In addition, it is important to understand that not only class origin or position, but also other sources of identity including race/ethnicity, regional origin, nationality, religion, gender, and sexual orientation overlap and intersect in the constitution of the identity of the "poor."

Fourth, avoiding a fixed curriculum, as is suggested in assumption 4, is clearly at odds with other suggestions in the document. For instance, the document states that "Dialogue is expected to generate around themes directly linked to survival skills. Thus the classes [will] serve not to assimilate, but accommodate, and introduce U.S. society and structure to the participants [sic]." Yet, a list of twelve themes is suggested for a twelve-week period of literacy training. These are (1) family/personal identification; (2) health and related issues; (3) jobs, rights, and responsibilities; (4) transportation, public and private; (5) education, children's rights and parent participation; (6) housing, rights and responsibilities; (7) banking and economics; (8) law and government; (9) emergency access and prevention; (10) shopping and consumer issues; (11) community resources; and (12) media and leisure time.

While a list of fairly generic themes, there is a tension between self-proclaimed participatory planning and these pre-selected topics. Furthermore, this preliminary selection of themes looks very similar to the practices of many traditional ESL programs. Indeed, this pre-determined list of "generative themes" is antithetical to the methods and spirit of critical teaching. A generative theme is an existential and crucial daily life situation for members of a given "oppressed" community. When a generative theme is discovered through thematic investigation and is codified, it becomes a knowable object mediating between knowing subjects, and it then leads to discovering "generative words" (selected based on their syllabic complexity and richness), the basis for the Freirean literacy training process (Torres, 1992a, 1992b). In the Freirean model it is the group itself, with the critical intervention of teachers as facilitators, that should generate the themes of study (Freire, 1970, 1985).

The comprehensive assumptions of the El Refugio project are based on a voluntaristic, romantically populist, and perhaps traditional approach; yet there are enough seeds in the program for a potentially innovative popular education approach. Unfortunately, the "militant" discourse prevailing in the program documents, while attempting to be popular-oriented, and perhaps monolithic in ideological terms, has obscured differences and emerging conflicts. Nevertheless, despite some political and pedagogical flaws, program outcomes have shown remarkable gains in literacy training (Pruyn and Fischman, 1994).

As the program has changed, what has been particularly relevant to this discussion has been a change in the program's intellectual orientation. It has moved from an inflammatory rhetoric to a discourse closer to the needs of and more accessible to the people who participate in the program. These changes in the program took place when the leadership of the program embraced the epistemological principles of popular education as an educational process that could not be predetermined or based on prescribed recipes.

Change was not easy. The leadership had sharp exchanges among themselves; teachers felt a lack of control over the teaching and learning process; students, drawing from their previous experience in schooling, asked for traditional and "safe" lessons rather than experimental approaches or a curriculum based on "generative themes"; and external pressures to the program also ran high.

After the initial shock, students and teachers began a contradictory and dynamic journey toward changing their supposedly "popular education" literacy lessons. Curriculum reform has been clearly understood as a way of formulating a literacy program embedded in the everyday struggle for changing the living conditions of Central American immigrants. This curriculum reform has aimed to help them to cope with, but also to understand their everyday life as Latinas and Latinos in the U.S., and particularly in the city of Los Angeles. A curriculum is being developed that takes the goals, aspirations, and expectations of students into account and considers the students not as "abstract" immigrants, but as women and men; as members of different ethnic groups; as lovers of different books, foods, and sports.

When the program shifted from a paternalistic and self-assured popular education discourse to an educational process of struggle and participation—in the best tradition of the rebellious history of popular education—this facilitated everybody in criticizing, resisting, and contesting through a pedagogy of questioning the sacred truths of the old literacy program. As this has occurred, El Refugio de Los Angeles has become a place of reading and transforming the word and the world.

Buenos Aires, Argentina: Native Popular Education. Free and mandatory public education of a relatively high quality has been an important part of the making of Argentina as a nation. The education of the native population has been part of a compulsory public schooling project developed by liberal states since the last quarter of the nineteenth century. However, the quantity and quality of the services for native communities have always been extremely poor, both in themselves and in comparison to school programs for non-native populations.

Educational discrimination against natives has historical and structural roots in Latin America. While native populations endure social and economic discrimination comparable to the most impoverished sectors of the rural and urban areas in the region, they have also been subject to other forms of discrimination—a form of double jeopardy—based on their ethnic origin. They are further oppressed because of their distinctive culture and the history of colonization in the region. In short, they are doubly discriminated because they are poor and natives (Fischman and Hernandez, 1990, 1991, 1992).

Despite this situation, a small group of university researchers, students, and members of a Mapuche community in the Province of Buenos Aires, Argentina, managed to developed four community-based programs that were designed and implemented using action technologies, including popular education and participatory action research.

The Mapuche community is located 350 kilometers from the city of Buenos Aires, the cosmopolitan capital of Argentina. The Mapuches were among the original inhabitants of the region, yet this Mapuche community is the only native community that has survived in the area. Even though this community of Mapuche has been described as being completely acculturated in that they are monolingual in Spanish, 95 percent Catholic, and most have attended elementary school, the nonindigenous inhabitants of the region perceive them as ethnically different. They are still seen as Indians or Mapuche people.

The community settlement is located in one of the richest and most productive soils in the world. However, in order to remain in this area, the Mapuche community has lost almost all of its visible ethnic characteristics, such as the Mapuche language (Mapundungun), sociopolitical and economic organizational systems, religious practices, handicrafts, and their trademark clothing (Hernandez and others, 1993).

As a means of ethnic recognition, in 1989 the school district set up a bilingual education program and implemented the celebration of the "Native Day." This bilingual program did not include community participation nor was it taught or managed by Mapuches. Lack of first nation people's participation was a basic trait of almost all social and organizational actions toward improving community welfare—whether initiated and managed by the state or originated by the private sector. Since many welfare policies were devised, planned, and implemented without the Mapuche community participation, many of these initiatives were based on naive ideas about the ethnic and social characteristics of the Mapuche's culture.

In that context, the research team from the University of Buenos Aires began to develop a program with the community, including showing films of Mapuche life in other parts of the country. These activities triggered a vast array of reactions, and some members of the community asked for assistance from the research team. After a six-month period (which included informal meetings, workshops, and constant personal communications), a fairly representative group of community members and researchers agreed on a basic scheme for collaboration encompassing four participatory programs. These programs included improvement of the piglet livestock; revitalization of the Mapundungun (Mapuche) language; recovery of the traditional weaving techniques; and audiovisual and organizational techniques for recording community information. What follows is a brief description of one program, the recovery of traditional weaving techniques. This program illustrates some of the challenges that participatory decision-making and popular educators face.

The story begins with Mapuche women, who were deeply impressed when they realized that for more than fifty years they had not worked with their traditional handicraft weaving techniques. A small group of women daydreamed the possibilities of again using traditional Mapuche weaving techniques. As one of the Mapuche woman noted, their concern and excitement was "about the beauty of recovering their lost culture." Once the learning purpose was established, the researchers asked the community their opinion about how to carry out a workshop that would help recover the techniques and what organizational design was needed. The Mapuche community was enthusiastic but also fearful about the real chances of achieving these ambitious goals. Their fears clearly expressed doubts about their community's capability of learning the weaving techniques and implicitly, the ability of native but not certified teachers to teach them.

Their first challenge was finding native master handcrafters in other remote Mapuche communities in Argentina and bringing them to work in the community. The majority of the Mapuche nation is located in the South of Argentina, in the Patagonia region, 3,500 kilometers from this particular Mapuche community. The research team was in charge of searching for weaving teachers, while the community was in charge of planning aspects of their stay such as housing, food, and materials. Three Mapuche women master handcrafters were hired, and after a nine-month period, including three self-managed weaving workshops of one month each, the native women of the community recovered their weaving techniques. Not only did they learn their craft, but they also developed a production cooperative that sold their products in the market, becoming an example to both native and non-native communities alike.

Despite the fact the program was developed for cultural rather than economic purposes, the workshops resulted in a lucrative source of income for the community. These workshops and later the production cooperative created the conditions for self-reflection. They challenged the women's traditionally dominated roles and their powerless position both within and outside the community. When the visiting master handcrafters left, the women in the weaving workshop decided that one of them—the best artisan—would be their new teacher.

With sales increasing and the quality of the products improving, school teachers from a nearby city asked to start a similar workshop in the city in order to learn the Mapuche weaving technique. The cooperative was puzzled by the request: non-natives wanting to learn a native skill? Moreover, those who wanted to learn were public school teachers who were teaching the community children. The Mapuche women were clear that these urban teachers would be in a better position to manufacture and sell weaving products than themselves. After an intense debate about who should be able to teach what, when, where, and to whom, the master teacher was appointed as teaching assistant in this school. However, she refused to go to the city and teach nonnatives, and the teachers eventually forgot about their request and lost interest in the activity (Hernandez and others, 1993).

The weaving cooperative is still in operation and has expanded to include other adult women as well as men and children. Men do not work as weavers, but they participate in all the auxiliary tasks, such as preparation of raw wool. During the entire process the research team did not intervene in organizational matters, but participated only when the community requested technical assistance and to set up a model of permanent self-evaluation.

This program was implemented after two years of complex ideological, cultural, and organizational processes. During this time, members of the native community and research team operated within a framework of basic agreements eventually conceptualized as the transference contract. The transference contract was a complex set of collective actions agreed upon by community members and the research team. It included among others things the need to build a climate of mutual trust, identify collective problems, agree on common strategies and solutions, and recognize that different ways of seeing, understanding, and changing the world exist.

Learning from Experience: Afterthought

From the incoherent post-modernity of Los Angeles to the snobbish style of Buenos Aires, we have followed two different pedagogical practices identified as popular education. This journey reveals a contemporary social and pedagogical phenomenon that can be summarized as follows: we can learn from conflict and from the incredible liberatory energies resulting from action technologies inextricably linked to democratic participation. This is perhaps a synthesis of what popular education is all about.

The symbolic power and enormous political potential of popular education rests on its invitation to self-criticism and epistemological awareness. As such, popular education will challenge all forms of domesticating pedagogical practices. These two stories suggest that contemporary societies should consider diverse forms of political, civic, and social representation through action technologies. In so doing, new political spaces will be created to accommodate new forms of political and educational participation and representation taking into account the heterogeneity of voices and identities—the notion of otherness.

El Refugio demonstrates that because of popular education's overriding concern to understand and change the world, it cannot be reduced to logical argument or reasoning. Freire argues: "As an educator I give much more emphasis to the comprehension of a rigorous method of knowing. Still we must ask ourselves, to know in favor of what and therefore, against what to know; in whose favor to know, and against whom to know. Those questions which we pose to ourselves as educators, bring us to the confirmation of another obviousness which is the political nature of education" (Freire, 1986, p. 97).

What is the legacy of popular education? To promote critical and democratic participation by concerned groups in every instance of decision making. Popular education does not claim a place exclusively as socialist education, nor can it be reduced to the myriad micro-educational efforts with disenfranchised populations. It can be embedded in any emancipatory project within such diverse contexts as state or nongovernment organizations, a large public school in New York, a small community in the Amazon or rural settings of the Appalachian mountains.

The Mapuche people in Argentina offer an example of the multiplicity of problems arising from multiple disqualifications and discriminations based on the notion of "otherness." "Other" then—whether it indicates gender, ethnicity, race, class, or sexual orientation—sets individuals apart in class categories, which, in the end, undermine community-building and notions of unity in difference. Working with poor and disenfranchised people causes popular education practitioners to be keenly aware of the complexity of human situations. More often than not, their radicalism is nourished by a sense of moral indignation—an ethical sense that propels them to find practical and efficient strategies for change. As Morrow and Torres point out, "While we may not be able to conceptualize entirely the multiple parallel determinations, or the interplay of class, race and gender in education, we can at least try to support the struggle to overcome discrimination, oppression, and the deep structuring of subjectivities with classist, racist and gender-biased overtones. This struggle has had a long history, and many anonymous heroes. This is not the time to romanticize the struggle, but neither is it a time to nurture historical amnesia" (Morrow and Torres, 1994, p. 61).

Popular education as an early form of action technology has a long and illustrious history. Projects have drawn on principles of participation and critique to fight historical and political amnesia while trying to read the word and the world. For popular education, this is the ultimate challenge.

References

Apple, M. *Official Knowledge: Democratic Education in a Conservative Age.* New York: Routledge, 1993.

Fischman, G., and Hernandez, I. "Educación Popular y Movimientos Indigenas." *Revista Argentina de Educación,* 1990, *9* (2), 67–79.

Fischman, G., and Hernandez, I. "Indigenous Movements, Ethnic Especificity and Education in Latin America." *New Education,* special issue, 1991.

Fischman, G., and Hernandez, I. "Educación, Etnicidad y Movimientos Indigenas en America Latina." In *Nuevo Proyecto.* Buenos Aires: Centro de Estudios para el Proyecto Nacional, 1992.

Freire, P. "The Adult Literacy Process as Cultural Action for Freedom." *Harvard Educational Review,* 1970, *40* (2), 205–225.

Freire, P. *Pedagogy of the Oppressed*. New York: Seabury Press, 1974.

Freire, P. "Educação. O Sonho Possivel." In C. Rodriguez Brandao (ed.), *O Educador Vida e Morte*. Rio de Janeiro: Edições Graal, 1980.

Freire, P. *The Politics of Education: Culture, Power, and Liberation*. Westport, Conn.: Bergin & Garvey, 1985.

Giroux, H., and McLaren, P. *Critical Pedagogy: The State and Cultural Struggle*. Albany: State University of New York Press, 1989.

Hernandez, I., Calcagno, S., Fischman, G., Canamasas, B., Comaleras, D., and De Jong, I. *La Identidad Enmascarada: Los Mapuche de Los Toldos*. Buenos Aires: Editorial de la Universidad de Buenos Aires, 1993.

Kozol, J. *Illiterate America*. New York: Plume Press, 1985.

Morrow, R., and Torres, C. A. "Education and Reproduction of Class, Gender, and Race: Responding to the Postmodern Challenge." *Educational Theory*, 1994, *44* (1), 43–63.

Pruyn, M., and Fischman, G. "De nosotros sale nada: The Social Construction of Critically Informed Pedagogy in Los Angeles." Paper presented at the annual meeting of the American Educational Research Association, New Orleans, Apr. 1994.

Stelck, B. F. "Knowledge Transfer and Reciprocity: A Canadian Theological Education Project in Kenya." Doctoral dissertation, University of Alberta, Edmonton, Canada, 1994.

Torres, C. A. *The Church, Society, and Hegemony: A Critical Sociology of Religion in Latin America*. (R. A. Young, trans.) Westport, Conn.: Praeger, 1992a.

Torres, C. A. "Participatory Action Research and Popular Education in Latin America." *International Journal of Qualitative Studies in Education*, 1992b, *5* (1), 51–62.

Torres, C. A. "Paulo Freire as Secretary of Education in the Municipality of Sao Paulo, Brazil." *Comparative Education Review*, 1994, *38* (2), 181–214.

Torres, R. M. "Una Conversación con Paulo Freire." *Educación Popular*. Ecuador: Centro de Estudios de la Comunicación, 1986.

CARLOS ALBERTO TORRES *is professor in the Graduate School of Education as well as assistant dean for student affairs and coordinator of comparative and topical programs, Latin American Studies, at the University of California, Los Angeles. He is from Argentina.*

GUSTAVO FISCHMAN *is assistant professor at the Universidad de Lujan, Provincia de Buenos Aires, Argentina.*

The annotated references in this chapter have been developed by this volume's authors to help readers explore action technologies that interest them more deeply.

Action Technology Resources: An Annotated Bibliography

Ann Brooks, Karen E. Watkins

Action technologies are varied and adaptable to unique situations and contexts. Many excellent resources are available to help both practitioners and scholars develop appropriate approaches and methodologies for making change through action inquiry. Selected references are described below. References are categorized by action technology rather than alphabetically.

Action Learning

McGill, I., and Beaty, L. *Action Learning: A Practitioner's Guide.* London: Kogan Page, 1992.

    This guide for implementation shows people how to plan and use action learning in programs where each person pursues his or her own problem in sets, using peers in the set for individual learning.

Marsick, V. J. "Action Learning and Reflection in the Workplace." In J. D. Mezirow and Associates, *Fostering Critical Reflection in Adulthood: A Guide to Transformative and Emancipatory Learning.* San Francisco: Jossey-Bass, 1990.

    This chapter reports research on the Scandinavian model of action reflection learning developed by the Management Institute, Lund, Sweden.

Marsick, V. J., and Cederholm, L. "Developing Leadership in International Managers: An Urgent Challenge!" *The Columbia Journal of World Business,* 1988, 23 (4), 3–11.

    This article provides a review of various models of ARL and their unique fit to the development of global managers.

Mumford, A. *Management Development: Strategies for Action.* London: Institute of Personnel Management, 1989.

A long-time advocate and practitioner of action learning, Mumford describes a wide range of informal approaches to managerial learning that include, and are based upon, action learning principles.

Pedler, M. (ed.). *Action Learning in Practice.* (2nd ed.) Aldershot, England: Gower, 1991.

This collection provides first-hand examples and perspectives on the planning and implementation of action learning programs in England.

Revans, R. W. *The Origin and Growth of Action Learning.* Bickley, England: Chartwell-Bratt, 1982.

This collection of articles and reports by Revans is a must for those interested in the history and use of action learning.

Action Research

Chisholm, R., and Elden, M. "Features of Emerging Action Research." *Human Relations,* 1993, *46* (2), 275–298.

Summarizes current thinking and research on action research and introduces five articles that deal extensively with new thinking in action research where the goal is participant meta-learning as well as problem-solving. These articles constitute a special issue of *Human Relations* on emerging varieties in action research. Useful introduction and overview of new ideas and methods in action research in an organizational context.

Cunningham, J. B. *Action Research and Organizational Development.* Westport, Conn.: Praeger, 1993.

This, the best of the recent books on action research, offers the practical guidelines and insights of an experienced action researcher. The book introduces action research—defining what it is and where it came from, and describing different approaches. Two main sections follow, suitably titled "Research" and "Action."

Emery, F., and Thorsrud, E. *Democracy at Work.* Leiden, Netherlands: Nijhoff, 1976.

The basic report of the Norwegian Industrial Democracy Program, at the time the largest known action research program, written by the program's two main architects. Shows their larger overall political and societal change strategy as anchored in specific, company-based action research projects. This is the source of the ideas for democratizing action research.

Kemmis, S., and McTaggart, R. (eds.). *The Action Research Planner.* Geelong, Australia: Deakin University Press, 1982.

This small readable volume is oriented predominantly to teacher staff development. In it, the action research cycle is described, illustrated, and broken down into guidelines for conducting the action research project. Helpful information includes steps in action research, a topic matrix, and research tips.

Kemmis, S., and McTaggart, R. (eds.). *The Action Research Reader.* Geelong, Australia: Deakin University Press, 1988.

This is an excellent collection of classic and more recent articles on action research. From Kurt Lewin and his inaugural action research studies to more contemporary variants of action research, the volume is both historically interesting and useful.

Action Science

Argyris, C. *Reasoning, Learning, and Action: Individual and Organizational.* San Francisco: Jossey-Bass, 1982.

The appendix of this practical book introduces the term *action science.* The book contains many examples of case work, sample maps, and Argyris' comments on cases.

Argyris, C. *Knowledge for Action: A Guide to Overcoming Barriers to Organizational Change.* San Francisco: Jossey-Bass, 1993.

Argyris' most recent volume reads almost like a novel. It chronicles his work over a five-year period with a consulting organization. This is an excellent resource for those who want to see how action science works.

Argyris, C., Putnam, R., and Smith, D. M. *Action Science: Concepts, Methods, and Skills for Research and Intervention.* San Francisco: Jossey-Bass, 1985.

One might think that this would be the best statement of the nature of action science, but it is actually more useful for scholars than practitioners. The book presents the theoretical origins of action science, describes how it differs from other forms of research, and explains how action science is practiced. This book is tough going for most people.

Argyris, C., and Schön, D. A. *Theory in Practice: Increasing Professional Effectiveness.* San Francisco: Jossey-Bass, 1974.

This volume remains one of the clearest descriptions of the theory of action science. Based on Argyris' and Schön's work with school administrators, the book describes how they worked with this group, presents the theory underlying that work, and illustrates action science practice.

Watkins, K. E., and Marsick, V. J. *Sculpting the Learning Organization: Lessons in the Art and Science of Systemic Change.* San Francisco: Jossey-Bass, 1993.

This book describes how organizations can create continuous learning and empowerment through the use of action technologies and other systemic change strategies. Both philosophically and practically, the book is written from an action science perspective. Adult educators and trainers will find this a readable book about action science targeted specifically to them.

Collaborative Inquiry

Group for Collaborative Inquiry. "Democratizing Knowledge." *Adult Education Quarterly*, 1993, *44* (1), 43–51.

In "Democratizing Knowledge," the Group for Collaborative Inquiry lays out the ideological underpinnings for collaborative inquiry.

Reason, P. (ed.). *Human Inquiry in Action: Developments in New Paradigm Research*. London: Sage, 1988.

This book describes several applications of collaborative inquiry. It also gives specific advice based on Reason's and others' experience of working with graduate students and others in collaborative inquiry groups.

Reason, P., and Rowan, J. (eds.). *Human Inquiry: A Sourcebook of New Paradigm Research*. Chichester, England: Wiley, 1981.

In this book, a range of authors discuss their approaches to collaborative and other forms of non-positivist research.

thINQ. "Phenomenology as an Interpretive Frame: The Evolution of a Research Method for Understanding How Learning Is Experienced in Collaborative Inquiry Groups." In *35th Annual Adult Education Research Conference Proceedings*. Knoxville: University of Tennessee, 1994.

This paper examines the philosophical approaches that ground the methodology. In particular, it examines how collaborative inquiry draws on both phenomenology and heuristic inquiry, but extends them to group inquiry.

Participatory Action Research

McTaggart, R. "Principles for Participatory Action Research." *Adult Education Quarterly*, 1991, *41* (3), 168–187.

This excellent article summarizes the distinguishing features of participatory action research.

Whyte, W. *Participatory Action Research*. Newbury Park, Calif.: Sage, 1991.

This edited volume is a more recent work by this long-term action researcher. Descriptions of different types of action research are offered as well as contrasts among them. Earlier volumes by Whyte portray book length descriptions of Whyte's action research projects and might also be of interest.

Popular Education

Escobar, M., Fernandez, A. L., and Guevara Niebla, G., with Freire, P. *Paulo Freire on Higher Education: A Dialogue at the National University of Mexico*. New York: State University of New York Press, 1994.

This conversation with Paulo Freire is a rich testimony to the contradictions and possibilities of radical theoretical paradigms in the realm of higher education. The book offers new insights into the implementation of popular education outside nonformal settings.

Gadotti, M. *Reading Paulo Freire*. New York: State University of New York Press, 1994.
This book is the most up-to-date and straightforward analysis of Freire's life and work, written from the perspective of one who collaborated with Freire. The author played a pivotal role in developing the notion of public popular schooling, that is, the application of popular education principles within formal school settings.

McLaren, P., and Lankshe, C. (eds.). *Politics of Liberation: Paths from Freire*. London: Routledge, 1994.

McLaren, P., and Leonard, P. (eds.). *Paulo Freire: A Critical Encounter*. London: Routledge, 1993.
These two books provide a valuable basis for discussing the work of Paulo Freire from theoretical, epistemological, and empirical perspectives. The articles explore the work of Freire both in the Third World and in advanced industrialized societies, showing ways of seeing and implementing popular education appropriate to the particular context.

Torres, C. A. *The Politics of Nonformal Education in Latin America*. New York: Praeger, 1990.
This book is an indispensable source of analysis of theories, methodologies, and practical experiences of popular education in Latin America. It includes cases from Brazil, Chile, Mexico, Nicaragua, Grenada, and Cuba.

Torres, C. A. *Estudios Freireanos*. Buenos Aires: Ediciones del Quirquincho, 1994.
For those who read Spanish, Torres's book offers a systematic appraisal of popular education as public policy in Brazil from 1989 to 1992, during Paulo Freire's administration as Secretary of Education in the state of São Paulo, Brazil.

Youngman, F. *Adult Education and Socialist Pedagogy*. London: Croom Helm, 1986.
Youngman's book presents an incisive analysis of the limits and possibilities of popular education and radical adult education in diverse contexts. It includes analyses of principles of adult learning from non-conductist approaches, and adult education as a socialist pedagogy in China, Mozambique, and Botswana.

ANN BROOKS *is assistant professor in the Adult Education and Human Resource Development Program, University of Texas at Austin, and a member of the Group for Collaborative Inquiry.*

KAREN E. WATKINS *is associate professor of adult education, University of Georgia, and former director of the graduate program in human resource development, University of Texas at Austin.*

*This chapter summarizes this volume and suggests points of compari-
son among the different action technologies, discusses issues of validity
among action technologies, and offers a number of implications for
adult and continuing education practitioners regarding the use of
action technologies.*

A Framework for Using Action
Technologies

Karen E. Watkins, Ann Brooks

In this volume, we have explored action technologies that enhance action and
learning: action research, action-reflection learning, action science, collaborative inquiry, participatory action research, and popular education. Each of these
technologies offers adult and continuing educators a unique approach to
changing individuals, groups, organizations, and societies. Whether the adult
educator is interested in social change or personal and professional development, action technologies may guide the process. In this chapter, we compare
the different action technologies, discuss issues of validity when thinking about
action technologies as research, and conclude with a discussion of the uses of
action technologies in adult and continuing education.

A Comparison of the Action Technologies

All of the action technologies as described in these chapters aimed at change.
In action research, people used data to inform the way work was organized. In
action-reflection learning, people learned how to learn from their experience to
act more effectively. In action science, people examined their experience to see
patterns of learning or meta-learning, and thus, to change their behavior. The
scholar practitioners using collaborative inquiry reflected critically on systematically gathered data and their own experience to examine an issue of mutual
concern. Popular educators facilitated groups in naming their own problem and
developing their own solutions in the context of oppression. Participatory action
research is similar to popular education, though it is often more structured. In
all cases, these insights led people and organizations to design action in new
ways. We discuss each of the action technologies from this volume below.

NEW DIRECTIONS FOR ADULT AND CONTINUING EDUCATION, no. 63, Fall 1994 © Jossey-Bass Inc., Publishers

Action Research. Action research, the first formalized action technology, grew out of the belief that people would take more effective action by collecting and analyzing data together. Looking at the facts of the context would "unfreeze" people's understanding and help them learn. People see the need for change as they collect data around a problem, feed it back to the organization, and decide on solutions. Action research as a technology typically includes:

1. Formation of groups from among those who have the problem
2. Reflection on problems in groups
3. Collection of data around the problems
4. Group analysis and group feedback
5. Group-designed interventions to attempt to solve the problem.

Action research is an iterative, cyclic process of intervening, collecting data on the effectiveness of the intervention, reflecting on results, and designing new interventions.

Max Elden and Reidar Gjersvik illustrated the evolution of action research in Chapter Three by describing changes that have taken place in Norway's workplace democracy program. From a predominantly researcher-driven technology, action research has grown to a more collaborative, participant-driven technology. Symbolic of this shift is the current use of the word co-researchers in place of the traditional research term "subjects." This has meant that at least in Norway, co-researchers have become collaborators not only in providing the research site and implementing the solutions suggested by the data, but in directing the research process as well. This means they define the problem, collect and analyze the data, and determine the appropriate action to take. Elden and Gjersvik pointed out that in Norway, this move to share control over the actual research process with the co-researchers is part of an explicit move to democratize work life. This means that action research in Scandinavia is part of a broader move to place control over work in the hands of those doing the work.

Action-Reflection Learning. Reg Revans, the father of action learning—also called action-reflection learning—suggests that people learn best when focused on real problems in their own work and lives. Through work in sets that strongly resemble action research teams, participants, who typically come from very diverse contexts, examine and work on solutions to the different problems each of the members are facing. Problems must be meaningful, which typically means that they are challenging work assignments. Success or failure is highly visible. Group reflection is again a hallmark.

People do not typically ask questions that challenge their pet assumptions. In order to challenge these assumptions, action-reflection learning teams bring the perspectives of "strangers" to the tasks of problem-setting and problem-solving in order to heighten the team's ability to probe below their surface with penetrating questions. Teams do not include experts who tell the problem-holder what to do because this prevents discovery learning and may not lead to fresh solutions. The non-expert can ask the "dumb questions" that often lead to new insights. Teams may also work on problems for departments and organizations of which they are not a part, and of which they have little prior knowledge.

O'Neil and Marsick in Chapter Two described their work with action reflection learning and illustrated the emphasis on developing fresh insights and on reframing the original problem with work they conducted at AT&T. In this action technology, we can see the stress being placed on participant learning as a major outcome, with at least as significant a role as solving real organizational problems.

Action Science. Action science adds to each of the above the idea that we can have a science of interpersonal action. Action research focuses on solving a problem; action reflection learning on learning how to learn while we act; and action science on the reasons why we do not do what we say we want to do.

Action science begins with the belief that no one deliberately sets out to make mistakes, yet we often find that we cannot create the solutions we envision. We get stuck, often in habits that repeat themselves, yet we cannot see what we are doing wrong or how to change our behavior. Our behaviors are learned, highly skillful responses, many of which are automatic and not conscious. In action science, we identify predictable patterns in human interaction that lead us to error, and we learn to change our behavior to get the results we want. Action science helps people see their behavior from a systems view, that is, how their actions are shaped by culture and organizational expectations.

In Chapter Four, Watkins and Shindell describe the teaching of action science in a higher education setting. This action technology's hallmark is its capacity to catalyze personal and organizational transformation by changing how people see their situations. With this emphasis on cognitive shifts, it is also one of the most difficult action technologies to learn and to enact.

Collaborative Inquiry. While most action technologies aim at the construction of informal knowledge for the purpose of improving action, collaborative inquiry as practiced by the Group for Collaborative Inquiry and thINQ work specifically to construct formal knowledge. These groups, consisting of both practitioners and scholars, have moved beyond the traditional view of knowledge construction as the solitary and competitive practice of scholars. Both groups integrate the knowledge of both scholars and practitioners, value the power of group learning, and believe that knowledge is not the property of single individuals.

In the case of both groups, a problem or phenomenon of interest common to the research group is identified, and then in a process of reflecting on experience and action, they attempt to understand more deeply its structure or meaning. This differs from some other action technologies in this book in that the object of reflection is not necessarily intentional action, but the everyday lives and experiences of the participants. The results of these inquiries are then used both to bring a greater understanding to the immediate practice of group members, as well as a more insightful understanding to contribute to formal theory. Thus, unlike other action technologies, these groups struggle to formalize their understandings into articles, chapters, and professional presentations. Their experiences as presented in Chapter Five form a template against which others might test their own knowledge construction.

Participatory Action Research. This variant emphasizes egalitarian participation by a community of individuals who "participate" in a system which is experiencing a problem. The group identifies the problem and develops strategies to overcome it. Many times the group will take as its task the development of critical reflection skills of group members. Each person will select an action problem, collect data to learn more about the nature of the problem, reformulate the nature of the problem, and develop and implement solutions. The role of the group is to offer suggestions, critique, and support to the individual members as they explore their own issues. For example, groups of teachers may come together to help each other improve their practice by conducting action research experiments.

In Chapter Six, Nod Miller describes her unique use of action research which blends T-group technology with action research's focus on action and change. Miller's approach is, like many forms of action research, an idiosyncratic approach adapted to her adult education aims. It is less typical than many approaches to participatory action research because of its more psychological understanding of what it means to be participant-led. Often in participatory action research, participants guide the research, name the problems and learn, with help from an outside facilitator, to solve them. In Miller's approach, participants learn what their problem is in the context of an enactment, and then collectively learn how to solve it.

Popular Education. This approach, based on the work of Paulo Freire, works from the premise that social change is essential to solving the problems that plague members of oppressed groups. In this approach, action is undertaken concurrently with an emerging consciousness of systemic social, class, gender, and ethnic barriers to problem solving.

Carlos Torres and Gustavo Fischman in Chapter Seven describe how critical control over the process by the participants is to the successful use of popular education. They also illustrate how the imposition of any ideology on the process inevitably aborts the liberating potential of popular education. Of particular importance in this chapter are the cases, which show popular education used in the Latin American setting with which it is often associated, as well as in a large industrialized and fragmented city in the United States. This popular education approach is of particular importance as we come to grips with the multiplicity that is increasingly present in both urban and rural life in the United States.

Contrasting Action Technologies

What, then, do these approaches have in common? In an analysis of the work of eleven action researchers, Peters and Robinson (1984) identified five characteristics that appeared most often: action research was problem-focused, collaboratively conducted and participatory, action-oriented, an organic and cyclical process, and scientific. In these pages, we see that these characteristics persist, though with an evolving understanding of the nature of science. Less frequently cited characteristics Peters and Robinson identified were that action technology is normative, ethically based, experimental, reeducative, emancipatory, stresses group dynamics, and is naturalistic. These additional characteristics appear to have increasing importance among those action researchers whose work is reflected in this volume.

The action technologies described here also vary along a number of dimensions. Each depends to a greater or lesser degree on the skilled interventions of a facilitator trained in guiding critical reflection, collecting data, and implementing change; and each emphasizes action over reflection, or vice versa. Placed on a continuum of these dimensions, the various approaches might look like Figure 9.1. In Table 9.1, we present a comparison of these approaches.

What is perhaps most striking in these displays is the amount of similarity among the approaches, particularly at the ideological level. While their key strategies and arena of interest vary considerably, fundamental purposes align many of these action technologies. Each is directed at change and empowerment. While some variants remain rooted in scientific rationalism, most lean toward anti-positivist theoretical foundations. Given the variety among these technologies, it is difficult and probably undesirable to seek a common standard of effectiveness. Yet, how then do we move from practicing action technologies to evaluating their effectiveness? In the section which follows, we explore one of the fundamental dilemmas present in action technologies as a form of research: how to establish validity with so much variance in approach, context, and outcome.

Figure 9.1. Continua of Action Technologies

Table 9.1. A Comparison of Action Technologies

	Action Learning	Action Research	Action Science	Popular Education	Participatory Action Research	Collaborative Inquiry
Purpose	Management development	Organizational, social change	Individual, organizational change	Individual, community empowerment Social change	Individual, social change	Individual empowerment Knowledge production
Primary Level of Focus	Individual	Organization, society	Individual, organization	Society	Individual, society	Individual, discipline
Theoretical Foundations	Reflective and experiential learning theory	Scientific rationalism Experiential learning theory	Social psychology/organizational development Experiential learning theory	Dialectics Phenomenology	Critical theory	Phenomenology Feminism
Ideological Focus	Depends on the set facilitator	Efficiency, effectiveness	Model II	Liberation	Liberation	Democracy
Key Strategies	Group reflection "On demand" management training Focus on solving real problems	Group reflection Diagnostic research	Group critical reflection Directly observable data (cases) on the problems of interest	Group critical reflection Consciousness-raising strategies	Group reflection Focus on participant concerns	Group critical reflection Integration of data external to group and personal data

Assessing Validity in Action Inquiry

Those who use action technologies as a methodology of inquiry are often depicted more as interventionists or change agents than as researchers. However, this presents a dilemma if we are to use definitions of validity that have been developed for types of inquiry that have as their goal the description or explanation of reality. Thus, criteria developed to determine validity for other types of research are inappropriate for assessing the quality of action inquiry.

Because of the focus in action technologies on catalyzing change, we propose here change-focused criteria for judging validity in action inquiry. It is useful to compare these criteria to an established set of criteria from a more conventional research paradigm such as Lincoln and Guba's (1985) validity criteria for naturalistic inquiry. Table 9.2 presents these contrasts.

Table 9.1. (continued)

	Action Learning	Action Research	Action Science	Popular Education	Participatory Action Research	Collaborative Inquiry
Facilitator Role	Group process expert	Research-group expert	Action scientist	Process expert, researcher	Research-group expert	Coordinator or no facilitator
Research Aim	Informal organizational knowledge	Informal organizational and cultural knowledge	Informal individual, organizational knowledge Formal knowledge about organizational change	Informal cultural knowledge	Informal individual, cultural knowledge	Formal knowledge
Validity Criteria	Individual learning is enhanced Cost savings Organizational improvements	Problems are solved	Individuals, organizations transform their beliefs Future learning and problem solving is enhanced	Society is more literate, fair Participants are empowered	Problems are solved	Inquiry is credible, collaborative

The first criterion we have proposed is that of "skillfulness." In action inquiry, the skill of the interventionist or researcher is a key determinant in the quality of the results. Since the participants in action inquiry must produce the phenomenon they wish to study, the action inquirer who facilitates the inquiry must have a high level of interpersonal competence. This is true whether or not the facilitator is highly directive. Since the researcher and participants are the instruments in action inquiry, data on their practice must be obtained. The facilitator must typically do this while simultaneously observing, teaching, and helping others. This is because the facilitator is usually more concerned with the use of the technology as a form of research, while the participants are frequently more concerned with the practical results of the technology.

The facilitator must also be able to teach the participants new research and action skills. They must learn the tools of research appropriate to their chosen problem and also learn how to act differently in order to produce new results. Few action researchers appear to acknowledge the degree to which this action-taking is dependent on the ability of the participants to learn and apply new skills (Argyris and Schön, 1991). Action inquirers will not produce usable results without a facilitator who is skilled in teaching the new skills to organizational participants—or in creating a process through which participants can learn and teach each other new skills. Whether actively facilitated or internally

Table 9.2. Emerging Criteria for Validity in Action Research Compared with Guba and Lincoln's Validity Criteria for Naturalistic Inquiry

Guba and Lincoln (1985)	Action Research
Trustworthiness/credibility How can we establish confidence in the truth of the findings for both the context and the respondents?	*Skillfulness* How can we develop both action and research skills among ourselves and participants to ensure that the solution works in context?
Transferability/applicability How do we determine the extent to which the findings have applicability with other contexts or subjects?	*Relevancy/usability* How do we determine the relevance of findings to the needs of the problem context?
Dependability/consistency How do we determine whether the findings would be repeated with the same or similar subjects or contexts?	*System competency* To what extent are we able to determine the systemic fit of solutions so that problems are solved in a manner that permits ongoing system learning?
Confirmability/neutrality To what extent are the findings determined by the subjects and the conditions of the inquiry and not by the biases of the researcher?	*Normative consistency* How consistent are procedures and outcomes with the normative theory guiding the research? Do participants learn? Are situations transformed as predicted by the action technology model?

Source: Watkins, 1991.

driven, the action technology depends on the acquisition of new skills for knowledge creation and utilization.

Finally, facilitators of action technologies, at least in the newer more participative forms, must often face their own needs to control the process. A theme that emerges again and again in these chapters is that expert control over the production of knowledge is fundamentally at odds with the action inquiry process. This often means that facilitators must examine their own intentions to impose an ideology, reap ego-related or professional rewards, or achieve a "successful" outcome. This can be a painful process and is not one that many undertake willingly. Again, this form of internal critique is a new skill for many.

The second and third criteria, "usability" and "system competency," look beyond the participants in the process to ask whether or not the results of the process are usable or useful by the system of which they are a part and, beyond this, to whether or not the system as a whole is better off as a result of the actions taken (Cunningham, 1993; Argyris, 1970). System competency here is defined as an ability to continue to learn, to continue to cycle from idea to detection of new problems, to action and back again, iteratively improving the system's effectiveness. The system is bounded by the participants in the action research process, by their perceptions of what is inside and what is outside of the problem. One of the most interesting aspects of the popular education examples in this volume is the scope of the system they define. Yet, it is equally interesting in the participatory action research and collaborative inquiry chapters to see that a more internal system state, with very narrow boundaries, produces a deeper interior probing and ultimately enhanced system state.

The fourth criterion, "normative consistency," asks whether or not the procedures for changing individuals and systems were ethical, at least within the normative philosophy of the action researchers. This is fairly complex in practice since both the outside action technology facilitator and the inside participants undoubtedly have varying views about what is ethical in the service of change. Positions as disparate as "use whatever works" to "use only that which does no harm and obtain informed consent" are common in a group of action researchers. Argyris (1970) has consistently called for standards of openness, experimentation, and mutual free and informed consent. Freire (1982) stated: "We have to be very clear about the objective of this work: it is the people themselves, not the advancement of science. If, however, the people are silent, then we have to provoke them, because we are not neutral" (Kemmis and McTaggart, 1988, p. 272). In this criterion, internal consistency between ethic and action and consensus among participants are suggested. In effect, this lends support to Argyris' ideas that there must be openness and informed consent since these are prerequisite to achieving consensus. At a minimum, the action researchers' philosophy of change should be publicly disclosed and discussed.

Threats to Validity in Action Research. As we have both practiced action research and observed the examples given in these chapters, we have noted a number of problems in implementing action research effectively. We identify these as potential threats to validity in action research. In this section, we describe issues of validity of process over outcome, issues of skill, and theory to practice gaps.

Does validity of process or diagnosis necessarily produce validity of outcome? On the one hand, because diagnosis is easier to set up as a more "controlled" research process, the researcher often expends more time and energy in this area, leaving the actual implementation of the action recommendations to the participants who may or may not have acquired the skills to implement them. Whether or not the outcomes developed actually solve the presented problem, as in normal science research, is the most difficult criterion. Action inquirers have difficulty communicating the extent to which the interventions they implement are skillful, other than in terms of their outcomes. This probably accounts for the plethora of "success stories" among action research reports. Yet, most action inquiry projects are long-term, cyclical processes of successive approximations. Where are the critical reports of the more problematic fits and starts of such efforts? The skill of diagnosis and analysis in real time is difficult to communicate, but perhaps greater detail about the early stages of an action research project would help those who wish to use action technologies become acquainted with what is involved. However, in the end, skills using action technologies are highly personal. As Moustakas (1990) notes in paraphrasing Polanyi, "The synthesis of essences and meanings inherent in any human experience is a reflection and outcome of the researcher's pursuit of knowledge" (p. 33).

Is it a question of validity or of gaps in skill? As we reflect on our own practice, we are struck by what seems like a minimizing of the extraordinary difficulty in developing both one's own and participants' skill in enacting new behaviors suggested by the notions of validity presented here. Watkins recalls the supervisor who came in to one group session with his equivalent of a "Eureka!" He reported that he had tried to use the new skills he was learning to discipline an employee. He stopped himself from lapsing into one of his frequent temper flare-ups and remembered to listen to the employee and, while sharing his initial judgment about her behavior, to inquire into her reasoning about the incident. He found that his new skills made her much more receptive to his advice. In effect, he had learned a new way to control others, rather than a new paradigm for empowering others. He had a tool, but not the underlying values behind the tool. Despite his learning progress, there was still a significant gap between his intentions and his actions.

The extraordinary number of minute-to-minute judgment calls between action and inquiry imperatives may also lead to compromises of either or both agendas. In types of action inquiry such as action science, where the goal is to teach people new behaviors that are themselves difficult or highly threatening, the interventionist must continually respond to the evolving ability and willingness of the participant to change. Similarly, in action research, the highly revealing information about attitudes and perceptions in a work organization, which is often turned up in the process of data collection, can be extremely disruptive to the organization's status quo, upsetting formal and informal power relationships. Conducting research that might add to knowledge under these conditions is difficult and requires enormous skill.

Theory to Practice Gaps. Individuals seeking to solve problems in complex, real-time settings find that the problems change under their feet, often before the more in-depth iterative search for solutions suggested by action inquiry has achieved meaningful results. Gaps occur between theory or idea and action. For example, in a study of empowerment, Watkins and her colleague Bonnie Turner included in their initial contracting a requirement that all participants be volunteers. Midway in the process, a few individuals alluded to the process by which they "volunteered." Managers had called them into their offices or sent them a memo asking them to "volunteer" for this project. In other areas, a memo was sent to all supervisors asking that those interested contact personnel to sign up for the program. It became clear that leaving it up to the organization to determine how to solicit voluntary participation left room for many conceptions of the idea. In addition, part of the group structuring included a mixing of shifts and divisions; hence many groups included individuals from the areas that had mandated participation. This led to a number of discussions about the directly observable differences in empowerment from area to area in the organization, and feelings of injustice seemed to increase within those areas that had mandated participation. This is evidenced in comments like, "Well you can try that in *your* area, but in *our* area. . . ." While this situation creates a laboratory for learning about the impact of these differences within one organization, unless the learning leads to action to address the issue, system competence is not enhanced. The obvious contradictions between empowerment and mandatory participation had the potential to undermine the goals of this action research project.

Generalizability. Argyris and Lewin contend that the findings from action inquiry can add to the body of action knowledge, or in other words, the knowledge of action—outcome relationships. However, the facts that action inquiry is heavily bounded by time and space, dependent on the skills of the facilitator and participants, and has increasingly moved away from the methodology of experimental and natural science suggest that the notion of generalizability cannot be understood in the conventional way. Traditionally, generalizability depends upon the ability of the researcher to control the research setting in terms of who will participate in the study and what factors will be allowed to influence the results. In action inquiry, the purpose is to make change in dynamic and complex systems. Thus, such excessive control on the part of the researcher oversimplifies the system rather than assists in addressing it in all its complexity. A study's generalizability must then rest in the hands of those who participate in or read about the study, rather than in the study itself. The most we can say about these studies is that we have learned something about our own situations from reading about the situation of others. The attempt to use research to uncover universal truths that can be told as though they apply to all people for all time is naive in a quickly changing and highly diverse world.

Implications

Participants in action research programs expect to be treated not as objects or even subjects, but as co-researchers engaged in "empowering participation" and in "co-generative dialogue" between "insiders and outsiders" (Elden and Levin, 1991). In action research, truth is in the process of inquiry itself. Was it reflexive and dialectical? Was it ethical and collaborative? Did participants learn new research skills, attain greater self-understanding, or achieve greater self-determination? Did the research solve significant practice problems or did it contribute to our knowledge about what will not solve these problems? Were problems solved in a manner that enhanced the overall learning capacity of the individuals or system? These are the types of questions that must guide action research (Argyris, 1980). In 1947, Lewin wrote: "The research needed for social practice can best be characterized as . . . a comparative search on the conditions and effects of various forms of social action, and research leading to social action. . . . This by no means implies that the research needed is in any respect less scientific or 'lower' than what would be required for pure science in the field of social events. I am inclined to hold the opposite to be true" (pp. 150–151). We agree.

Using Action Technologies in Adult and Continuing Education

Whether working to develop new skills among adult learners, solving societal or organizational problems, or working to transform cultures, action technologies are an important tool for adult and continuing educators. Issues of literacy, empowerment, and change are ably addressed using these tools. Action technologies are particularly consistent with the philosophical orientation of many adult and continuing educators. The emphasis on group reflection and empowerment, and the aim of social action, which are hallmarks of these action technologies, are also issues that permeate adult education literature. In this book, we have offered a number of cases of adult education at work to show how these action technologies have been used. It remains in the hands of those who read this volume to explore the many additional ways these action technologies might yet be used.

References

Argyris, C. *Intervention Theory and Method.* Reading, Mass.: Addison-Wesley, 1970.
Argyris, C. *Inner Contradictions of Rigorous Research.* New York: Academic Press, 1980.
Argyris, C., and Schön, D. "Participatory Action Research and Action Science Compared." In W. F. Whyte (ed.), *Participatory Action Research.* Newbury Park, Calif.: Sage, 1991.
Cunningham, J. B. *Action Research and Organizational Development.* Westport, Conn.: Praeger, 1993.
Elden, M., and Levin, M. "Co-generative Learning: Bringing Participation into Action Research." In W. F. Whyte (ed.), *Participatory Action Research.* Newbury Park, Calif.: Sage, 1991.
Freire, P. "Creating Alternative Research Methods: Learning to Do It by Doing It." In B. Hall, A. Gillette, and R. Tandon (eds.), *Creating Knowledge: A Monopoly?* New Delhi, India: Society for Participatory Research in Asia, 1982.
Kemmis, S. "Action Research in Retrospect and Prospect." In S. Kemmis and R. McTaggart (eds.), *The Action Research Reader.* Geelong, Australia: Deakin University Press, 1988.
Kemmis, S., and McTaggart, R. (eds.). *The Action Research Planner.* Geelong, Australia: Deakin University Press, 1982.
Lewin, K. "Frontiers in Group Dynamics." *Human Relations,* 1947, *1* (2), 150–151.
Lewin, K. "Group Decision and Social Change." In G. E. Swanson, T. M. Newcomb, and E. L. Hartley (eds.), *Readings in Social Psychology.* New York: Henry Holt, 1952.
Lincoln, Y., and Guba, E. *Naturalistic Inquiry.* Newbury Park, Calif.: Sage, 1985.
Moustakas, C. *Heuristic Research: Design, Methodology, and Applications.* Newbury Park, Calif.: Sage, 1990.
Peters, M., and Robinson, V. "The Origins and Status of Action Research." *Journal of Applied Behavioral Science,* 1984, *20* (2), 113–124.
Revans, R. *The Origins and Growth of Action Learning.* Lund, Sweden: Studentlitteratur, 1982.
Watkins, K. "Validity in Action Research." Paper presented to the American Educational Research Association, ERIC, 1991.

KAREN E. WATKINS *is associate professor of adult education, University of Georgia, and former director of the graduate program in human resource development, University of Texas at Austin.*

ANN BROOKS *is assistant professor in the Adult Education and Human Resource Development Program, University of Texas at Austin, and a member of the Group for Collaborative Inquiry.*

INDEX

ORDERING INFORMATION

NEW DIRECTIONS FOR ADULT AND CONTINUING EDUCATION is a series of paperback books that explores issues of common interest to instructors, administrators, counselors, and policy makers in a broad range of adult and continuing education settings—such as colleges and universities, extension programs, businesses, the military, prisons, libraries, and museums. Books in the series are published quarterly in Spring, Summer, Fall, and Winter and are available for purchase by subscription and individually.

SUBSCRIPTIONS for 1994 cost $47.00 for individuals (a savings of 30 percent over single-copy prices) and $62.00 for institutions, agencies, and libraries. Please do not send institutional checks for personal subscriptions. Standing orders are accepted.

SINGLE COPIES cost $16.95 when payment accompanies order. (California, New Jersey, New York, and Washington, D.C., residents please include appropriate sales tax.) Billed orders will be charged postage and handling.

DISCOUNTS FOR QUANTITY ORDERS are available. Please write to the address below for information.

ALL ORDERS must include either the name of an individual or an official purchase order number. Please submit your order as follows:
   Subscriptions: specify series and year subscription is to begin
   Single copies: include individual title code (such as ACE 59)

MAIL ALL ORDERS TO:
   Jossey-Bass Publishers
   350 Sansome Street
   San Francisco, California 94104-1342

FOR SUBSCRIPTION SALES OUTSIDE OF THE UNITED STATES, contact any international subscription agency or Jossey-Bass directly.

OTHER TITLES AVAILABLE IN THE
NEW DIRECTIONS FOR ADULT AND CONTINUING EDUCATION SERIES
Ralph G. Brockett, Editor-in-Chief
Alan B. Knox, Consulting Editor

Statement of Ownership, Management and Circulation
(Required by 39 U.S.C. 3685)

(ISSN)

1A. Title of Publication	1B. PUBLICATION NO	2. Date of Filing
NEW DIRECTIONS FOR ADULT AND CONTINUING EDUCATION	0 1 9 5 2 2 4 2	9/23/94

3. Frequency of Issue	3A. No. of Issues Published Annually	3B. Annual Subscription Price
Quarterly	Four (4)	$47.00 (personal) $62.00 (institution)

4. Complete Mailing Address of Known Office of Publication (Street, City, County, State and ZIP+4 Code) (Not printer)

350 Sansome Street, 5th Flr, San Francisco, CA 94104-1342 (San Francisco Cnty)

5. Complete Mailing Address of the Headquarters of General Business Offices of the Publisher (Not printer)

(above address)

6. Full Names and Complete Mailing Address of Publisher, Editor, and Managing Editor (This item MUST NOT be blank)
Publisher (Name and Complete Mailing Address)

Jossey-Bass Inc., Publishers (above address)
Editor (Name and Complete Mailing Address)

Ralph G. Brockett, Dept of Tech and Adult Educ, Univ of Tennessee, 402 Claxton Addition, Knoxville, TN 37996-3400
Managing Editor (Name and Complete Mailing Address)

Lynn D. Luckow, President, Jossey-Bass Inc., Publishers (address above)

7. Owner (If owned by a corporation, its name and address must be stated and also immediately thereafter the names and addresses of stockholders owning or holding 1 percent or more of total amount of stock. If not owned by a corporation, the names and addresses of the individual owners must be given. If owned by a partnership or other unincorporated firm, its name and address, as well as that of each individual must be given. If the publication is published by a nonprofit organization, its name and address must be stated.) (Item must be completed.)

Full Name	Complete Mailing Address
Simon & Schuster, Inc.	PO Box 1172 Englewood Cliffs, NJ 07632-1172

8. Known Bondholders, Mortgagees, and Other Security Holders Owning or Holding 1 Percent or More of Total Amount of Bonds, Mortgages or Other Securities (If there are none, so state)

Full Name	Complete Mailing Address
same as above	same as above

9. For Completion by Nonprofit Organizations Authorized To Mail at Special Rates (DMM Section 424.12 only)
The purpose, function, and nonprofit status of this organization and the exempt status for Federal income tax purposes (Check one)

(1) ☐ Has Not Changed During Preceding 12 Months   (2) ☐ Has Changed During Preceding 12 Months   (If changed, publisher must submit explanation of change with this statement.)

10. Extent and Nature of Circulation (See instructions on reverse side)	Average No. Copies Each Issue During Preceding 12 Months	Actual No. Copies of Single Issue Published Nearest to Filing Date
A. Total No. Copies (Net Press Run)	1,756	1,273
B. Paid and/or Requested Circulation 1. Sales through dealers and carriers, street vendors and counter sales	434	132
2. Mail Subscription (Paid and/or requested)	717	646
C. Total Paid and/or Requested Circulation (Sum of 10B1 and 10B2)	1,151	778
D. Free Distribution by Mail, Carrier or Other Means Samples, Complimentary, and Other Free Copies	66	66
E. Total Distribution (Sum of C and D)	1,217	844
F. Copies Not Distributed 1. Office use, left over, unaccounted, spoiled after printing	548	429
2. Return from News Agents	0	0
G. TOTAL (Sum of E, F1 and 2—should equal net press run shown in A)	1,765	1,273

11. I certify that the statements made by me above are correct and complete

Signature and Title of Editor, Publisher, Business Manager, or Owner

[signature] Larry Ishii Vice President

PS Form 3526, January 1991   (See instructions on reverse)